MONUMENTAL PROVIDENCE
Legends of History in Sculpture, Statuary, Monuments and Memorials

Paul F.Caranci
Heather A. Caranci

MONUMENTAL PROVIDENCE
Legends of History in Sculpture, Statuary, Monuments and Memorials

By
Paul F. Caranci
&
Heather A. Caranci

Monumental Providence: Legends of History in Sculpture, Statuary, Monuments and Memorials.

Visit our website at www.StillwaterPress.com for more information.
First Stillwater River Publications Edition
ISBN-10: 0-692-35055-1
ISBN-13: 978069235055-3

Library of Congress Control Number: 2014959160

1 2 3 4 5 6 7 8 9 10
Written by Paul F. Caranci & Heather A. Caranci
Photographs by Heather A. Caranci except where noted
Cover design by Dawn M. Porter
Published by Stillwater River Publications, Glocester, RI, USA

Table of Contents

Section II – Public and Private Buildings

Chapter 24 – Prospect Terrace

Chapter 25 – Roger Williams National Park

Chapter 26 – Burnside Park

Chapter 27 – Garibaldi Park

Chapter 28 – Blackstone Blvd. Park

Chapter 29 – Abbott Park

Chapter 30 – Gano Street Park aka Slate Rock Park

Dedication
by Paul F. Caranci

As always, I dedicate this book to my family: My wife and best friend Margie, my son Matthew, my daughter and new collaborator Heather. Their unwavering love and support enables me to pursue my dreams and for that I am ever grateful. To my grandchildren Matthew Jr., Jacob, Vincent and Casey who provide a new incentive to write. I hope they will experience the same joy and happiness that life has provided me. To my mother Anne whose guidance and example molded me into what I am, and my father, Frank who, though now at rest in a far better place, taught me that anything worth doing is worth doing right. To my mother-in-law Carol, the quiet one, who just always seems to be in the right place to lend a helping hand. Finally, to my sister Linda and brother-in-law Dennis who sacrifice daily for the well-being and comfort of others.

Desmond Tutu once said, "You don't choose family, they are God's gift to you." God has truly blessed me with many gifts.

Dedication
by Heather A. Caranci

God's greatest blessing is family and it is with an enormity of gratitude that I dedicate this book to mine: My parents, Margie and Paul, who built a solid foundation for our family through their profound examples of love, faith and sacrifice and their interminable guidance and support; my brother, Matthew, who lifts my spirits and encourages me to remain ambitious and reach towards my goals; my Nana Carol and Grandma Anne for their sweet and gentle compassion provided in that special way so unique to grandmothers; my Papa, Frank, who is resting peacefully, yet from above, continues to toil as my special angel, no doubt proud that we continue his work; my nephews, Matthew, Jacob and Vinny who have grown to be amazing little men, each in their own unique way. Their spirited youth keeps me forever young at heart.

To my pride and joy, my son Casey, who has changed my life forever and in the best of ways. It's through his every kiss, hug and smile that I find my strength. I am proud and honored to be his mother and to have the privilege of watching him grow into such a strong and extraordinary boy. He inspires me in all I do. Few words can express the incredible bond we share and I look forward to the years to come being his mother, teacher and guide. Casey was my assistant in a substantial part of the search for statues and monuments helping me to capture many of the images that appear in this book. Watching his excitement build to a crescendo as we discovered each new work of art made this experience all the more incredible for me.

Finally, special thanks to my dad for the opportunity to be his co-author on this book, this has truly been amongst the most rewarding of experiences.

Acknowledgements

As with all things in life, this book required the assistance of a great many people without whom publication would not have been possible. We are grateful for the research assistance of Gwenn Stearn and Tracey Croce of the Rhode Island Archives; Tom Evans and Ann Gancz Teixeira of the State House Library, Louise Moulton, Stephanie Fortunato, Lynne McCormack, Randall Rosenbaum, Sarah Zurier, Fr. Robert Hayman, and Justin MacDonald all of whom provided invaluable research support and assistance gathering the images used throughout this book. We also express our gratitude to Paul Campbell and Dr. Patrick Conley for their written contributions and assistance with the editing process.

Foreword

Public monuments and sculpture have served as an artistic form of cultural memory since the dawn of civilization. Many of the more monumental expressions of this form of remembrance are familiar icons. The pre-historic Stonehenge, Egypt's Sphinx, The Eiffel Tower, or America's Statue of Liberty and the Washington Monument are obvious examples of this form.

Although Providence cannot boast a larger than life expression of monumental public art, our local landscape is, nevertheless, fortunate to be graced with an abundance of public art in many forms and representing the work of a number of talented artists.

One could argue convincingly that our local public art is underappreciated or simply unnoticed, but Paul F. Caranci, Rhode Island's Deputy Secretary of State for Policy and Planning and the author of three books on local history, in collaboration with his daughter Heather, seek to change that perception by raising the profile of the public art that surrounds us. Their new publication, *Monumental Providence: Legends of History in Sculpture, Statuary, Monuments and Memorials,* offers an updated and much more detailed treatment of an earlier work, *Hidden Treasure,* authored by the late Robert Freeman and Vivienne Lasky more than three decades ago.

Providence's visible heritage of public sculpture, monuments, and memorials is both rich in diversity, purpose, and physical composition. Interestingly, one of the first documented representations of this art form was a Turk's Head, fashioned in the early 19th century from wood, while one of the latest additions to our public art can be found at the State House, also in the form of a wood carved likeness, in this case of "People's Governor" Thomas Wilson Dorr. Granite and bronze were favored by artists in the late 19th and early 20th centuries, but more recently contemporary sculptors have utilized reinforced concrete as a medium for local public sculpture.

Our public monuments and sculpture follow trends seen in many other cities. Providence commemorates its heroic individual figures such as General Ambrose Burnside, Roger Williams, or Esek Hopkins. We memorialize the sacrifice of war as exemplified by the Soldiers and Sailors Monument (1871) or the World War I Monument

(1929). Some examples of our local public sculpture such as the Independent Man, perched atop the Rhode Island State House, offer a symbolic representation of freedom, strength and self-reliance. Others, such as the exquisite Carrie M. Brown Memorial Fountain at Burnside Park, seek to convey the personal loss of a life cut short. Indeed, Providence is blessed to have many examples of these varied forms.

Monumental sculpture in Providence has also adapted to the city's changing landscape. In some cases it has enhanced the viewing experience. In others it has diminished its intrinsic value. Kennedy plaza's Civil War Monument, dedicated in 1871, stood prominently among its low-rise surrounding buildings. Today, after being relocated three times, its prominence is somewhat belittled by the tall buildings that surround it. The elegant bronze statue of the city's most prominent mayor, Thomas A. Doyle, once adorned the busy intersection at Cathedral Square, but now is largely hidden from public view behind a grove of trees near the corner of Weybosset and Chestnut streets. Undoubtedly, the most dramatic example of landscape adaptation was the removal of the 115-foot tall World War I Memorial from its inaccessible location at Memorial Square—known by most locals as "Suicide Circle"—to a much improved landscaped oasis along the revitalized river walk. The Carancis *Monumental Providence* can be enjoyed both as a casual read and as a useful guide during a walking tour of the Downtown and its surrounding neighborhoods.

I am confident that the Carancis' book will enjoy wide appeal among historians, artists, and those members of the general public who are curious to learn more about these silent testimonials to our city's storied past. Perhaps their work will inspire historians in other cities and towns to carry out similar surveys of their public sculpture.

Paul R. Campbell
Archivist, City of Providence

Introduction

Public statuary as we think of it, according to the Rhode Island Historical Preservation and Heritage Commission's 1999 publication, *Outdoor Sculpture of Rhode Island*, first appeared in this state in the mid-1800s inspired by a European idiom. Greco-Roman in origin, these masterpieces flourished and the resulting statues, monuments and memorials that are now scattered throughout the City of Providence stand as a testament to the people, places and events that have had a profound impact on the shaping of the history of Rhode Island's capital city.

In addition to being home to the greatest number of sculptures in the state, the capital city also boasts home to the first statue installed at a public site in Rhode Island. A statue of Benjamin Franklin cast in zinc by Richard Greenough, depicting Franklin holding a scroll in his hand with a tri-corn hat tucked securely under his arm, was positioned in 1855 in front of the Franklin Lyceum building on Westminster Street. Upon demolition of the Lyceum in 1926 the statue was moved to the lobby of Citizens Bank at 87 Empire Street in the City. Its location today is somewhat of a mystery although the last time it was seen in 2010 it was shrouded in a coat of gold paint inside one of the branches of Citizens Bank. Providence sculptor Frances Hoppin remarked at the statue's impressive dedication ceremony, "This is the first public statue in Rhode Island! Let it be but the beginning of a phalanx of statues! Let our heroes, our poets, our statesmen, our philosophers, and our men of worth, live among us not only in the form of their achievements, but in monuments of iron and bronze and marble, adorning our streets and parks, perpetually preaching their virtues and telling us that they once lived and acted, and were flesh and blood like ourselves."[1] Hoppin's vision speaks to our reality as hundreds of examples dot the Rhode Island landscape with the City of Providence leading with its example of monumental fine art. Though most of the great monuments were placed from 1870 to the mid to end 1920s, figurative sculpture continues to be in demand, particularly in

---

[1] Historical Preservation & Heritage Commission, Rhode Island. *Outdoor Sculpture of Rhode Island*. Providence: RI Historical Preservation & Heritage Commission, 1999, p.6.

the capital city which is home to world renowned Rhode Island School of Design.

Some are architectural gems while others evoke wonderment and amazement. Still others defy most logical attempts at discernment. Yet each represents an era past and possibly forgotten by the casual observer if not for this lasting remembrance of what once was.

Perhaps the grandest of all Rhode Island monuments, according to some at the Rhode Island Historical Preservation and Heritage Commission, is the Soldiers and Sailors Monument in Downtown Providence's Kennedy Plaza (Originally located just outside Providence City Hall, the monument was moved to its present location in 1906.) "Its size, complexity, and even its cost are remarkable. It is programmatically complex, with over a dozen relief plaques, four larger-than-life figures, and one monumental figure. The monument is large in scale – the base alone is 32 feet high. And it was an expensive enterprise for a small state, costing $57,000" in 1871 dollars, exceeding the $50,000 budget by some 14%. These monuments to the past can be found in many places throughout Providence and take on a plethora of forms. War memorials dot the landscape of Providence from neighborhood street corners to public parks. These tributes range from simple plaques lain in stone to larger-than-life equestrian mounted generals whose efforts were so instrumental in the cause of American freedom and justice. They enhance the inside and the outside of the City's buildings and in some instances they are gracefully sculpted on the edifice itself.

From life-sized to the great and the small, monuments adorn our public parks, churches, colleges and universities, historic federal, state and municipal buildings, and roadsides. They are crafted in a variety of source material including marble, wood, iron, and stone. Some are formed by the skilled hands of artisans while others are carefully crafted in iron molds. Even cemeteries are purposed with the most amazing examples of funerary art. However, despite the many extraordinary examples of funerary throughout the cemeteries of Providence, space limitations do not allow for their inclusion in this book.

Regardless of the variety that defines these artistic and historical wonders, the purpose is singular; to identify and honor our

• • •

heroes and community values. Yet, some of these artistic masterpieces seem to hide in plain view with thousands of otherwise unsuspecting and pre-occupied passerby walking or riding past each day without even as much as a notice. Rhode Island School of Design Assistant Professor of Sculpture, Richard Jarden, noted the irony in 1980 when he wrote in his forward to *Hidden Treasure: Public Sculpture in Providence*, "…Public sculpture is very difficult to see. On an immediate level, what is going on around it, behind it and sometimes on it can be as engaging as, or often more engaging than, the sculpture itself. We pass by sculptures every day without noticing them because they are mute, frozen helplessly in time, while we have the ability to move, even to move away."[2]

Through a study of its monuments, we are also provided a glimpse into how the average citizens of Rhode Island's capital city have chosen to commemorate and remember yesterday's heroes and events.

Monumental Providence: Legends of History in Sculpture, Statuary, Monuments and Memorials presents a seldom-told history of Providence as interpreted through the City's many sculptures, both great and small. It is presented in a format meant to facilitate the reader's understanding of the purpose and meaning of each monument while at the same time allowing for the organization of a self-guided tour of the sites permitting each historic and artistic piece to come to life for the tourist. Monuments will be found on the pages of this book according to category of placement. For example, those placed on the grounds of colleges and universities appear in Section I while those located at federal, state and municipal buildings may be found in Section II, etc. Further, a photograph of each monument is included as is a narrative description containing, to the extent possible, information about the sculptor or artist who designed the work, when it was placed and dedicated by the City, its historical significance and other relevant or interesting facts about it.

Sit back now and enjoy this virtual tour of Monumental Providence.

---

[2] Hidden Treasures, p.8

Section I

Colleges & Universities

Chapter 1

Brown University

Providence, Rhode Island 02912

The Brown Campus is listed on the National Register of Historic Places.

THE HISTORY OF THE BROWN BEAR MASCOT

Theodore Francis Green may well be best remembered by the airport in the City of Warwick that bears the name of this former Rhode Island Governor and United States Senator. Few today may know however that he is also credited with being the first person to float the idea of adopting the bear as the University's official mascot. In fact, on January 20, 1904, just seven years after his graduation from Brown University, he hung a stuffed bear's head in the trophy room of the newly constructed Faunce House in hopes of promoting it as the University's official mascot. Green explained his choice of a bear saying, "While it may be somewhat unsociable and uncouth, it is good natured and clean. While courageous and ready to fight, it does not look for trouble for its own sake, nor is it bloodthirsty. It is not one of a herd, but acts independently. It is intelligent and capable of being educated if caught young enough. It is a good swimmer and a good digger, like an athlete who makes Phi Beta Kappa. Furthermore, its color is brown; and its name is Brown."[3]

Green's conceptual symbol of power and strength was very quickly popularized with the student body. Before long, bears were found etched on the pages of Liber Brunensis, Brown's oldest publication, in celebrated fight songs and at sporting events.

Initial attempts to find a suitable mascot had failed miserably. In 1902, Isaac Goff, a local real estate executive, presented a brown and white burro during halftime of a football game. Although lovable with its long ears and gentle nature, the animal proved too timid to be an effective mascot.

In 1905, a student committee charged with finding ways to build spirit and excitement for an Ivy League football game Brown was hosting against Dartmouth acquired a live bear cub named Dinks as a University mascot. Dinks, however, proved every bit as timid as the burro as he refused to exit his cage on game day. His cub mate Helen, on the other hand, had no such compunction and emerged from her cage to stare down the Dartmouth cheerleaders. Brown may have

[3] www.brown.edu/Administration/News_Bureau/Databases/Encyclopedia/search.php?serial=BO   From Martha Mitchell's Encyclopedia Brunoniana

lost the game, but the live-bear mascot tradition took hold. Several other bear cubs followed Helen over the ensuing years.

In 1921, a bear named Bruno died after ingesting poison while roaming outside its cage in the Biology lab. The class of 1922 quickly purchased the cub's brother, dubbed Bruno II, to be used as a spring day mascot. Also known as Brunonia, the cub grew to over 500 lbs. over the next seven years before being retired after the Thanksgiving Day game of 1928.

Maine Governor Louis J. Brann presented Bruno III to the Brown University President in 1936. This feisty female gained notoriety when she bolted from her cage during a football game against Connecticut. The crowd watched as she climbed a large elm tree that grew in the stadium. Initial efforts to coax her down proved more entertaining than the lopsided game on the field until, several hours later, a very unhappy cub was lured from the tree with an offering of milk and sugar. Snagged by the police, the snarling cub was taken away bringing her career as a mascot to an abrupt end.

Her future replacement, Bruno V, died suddenly in 1939. A "funeral" service drew hundreds of students, alumni and curiosity seekers to the College Green where trumpets blared Taps and flags flew at half-staff. The body was then taken by a station wagon draped in black for burial at the Aldrich Field. The fanfare surrounding the sudden loss of such a beloved symbol demonstrated Bruno's significance to campus culture.

The tradition of live bear mascots seems to have ended sometime in the late 1960s only to be replaced by dancing and cheer-leading students darning a bear suit. Beginning as early as 1922 and continuing through 1988, various bear statues emerged on campus. Those statues immortalize and continue the Brown mascot legend providing a living history of one of the most endearing symbols of Rhode Island's oldest educational institution.

THE BRESLAU BEAR FOUNTAIN

Taken by the beauty of the Breslau Bear Fountain and enamored by the bear that he envisioned as Brown University's first mascot, future Governor Theodore Francis Green gifted this copy of German sculptor Ernest Mortiz Geyger's statue to Brown. (Photo by Heather Caranci)

The man responsible for promoting the bear as Brown's mascot is also responsible for the first bear statue on the campus. Theodore Francis Green was lecturing in economics in Breslau, Germany when a bronze statue in front of the medieval town hall caught his eye. A fountain constructed in 1904 immortalized a bear perched on a tree stump seemingly lapping water with its outstretched tongue. A gentle tug on the bear's collar released a stream of drinking water from its nostrils that passersby could use to fill aluminum cups that dangled from the chains that bound the bear's paws. Green was taken by its beauty and enamored by what he envisioned as the future mascot of his alma matter.

Green contacted the sculptor, Ernest Mortiz Geyger, a German living in Florence and secured the necessary permissions to have a second casting of the fountain made for him. The completed work was shipped to New York later that year and Green gifted it to the University. The second casting of the Breslau fountain was dedicated in a sunken courtyard at the Faunce House in 1932.

During World War II, when the Poles occupied Breslau, most everything German was intentionally destroyed and the City remade into present-day Wroclaw. At some point during this transformation, the original Breslau bear fountain was lost making this copy at Brown the only remaining copy of Geyger's casting.

In 2001, the Breslau Bear was removed from the courtyard of the Faunce House to make room for the glass fountain that currently graces the area. The University restored the Breslau Bear and, after informing the residents of a grateful Wroclaw, installed it at its new location on McGee Street just north of the entrance of the Faculty Club.

THE BRONZE BRUNO

Zechariah Chafee made a reality of Green's vision of employing the bear as Brown's official mascot by encouraging a fellow alum to initiate a subscription for the casting of this statue. The resulting "Put a hair on the bear" fundraising campaign was an overwhelming success and resulted in The Bronze Bruno. (Photo by Heather Caranci)

In 1922 Brown University graduate Zechariah Chafee, class of 1880, heard that a suggestion made at the 15th reunion of the class of 1907 was rejected. Chafee felt that that suggestion, to gift a bronze bear to the University for use as an enduring mascot, was a good one that needed implementation. He encouraged fellow alum Herbert B. Keen (1907) to start a subscription among alumni and himself became the first contributor. Keen set an ambitious fundraising goal of $10,000 to cast a life-size replica of a Kodiak Brown Bear, but by commencement day only $800 had been raised.

As necessity is always the mother of invention, a new campaign slogan was developed. The "Put a hair on the bear" campaign encouraged alumni to subscribe a single hair for one dollar or an entire patch of hair for $100.00. This effort proved successful, and with the funding now secured, the Committee selected New York City animal sculptor Eli Harvey for the work.

Harvey unveiled his model of "Bruno," standing upright on its hind legs, during the 1923 commencement exercises with Herbert Keen extolling the bear's strength, fearlessness, hardihood and resistance to attack as virtuous examples to the graduates. "We maintain that those of our young men who follow the example of the bear in these respects" Keen said, "will make for better scholars than those who lack Bruno's qualities."[4] Following the ceremony, the model was taken with much fanfare to the Gorham Manufacturing Company for casting which took place on August 18th.

Despite some wanting the statue to be placed on the site of the unveiling at the south end of the middle campus, the bronze was ultimately positioned in front of Marvel Gym at a dedication ceremony held in 1928. The bear stands on a pedestal that contains a piece of slate rock that, according to legend, was the stepping stone used by Roger Williams upon his arrival in the area he later named Providence.

The inscription on one side of the pedestal reads, "This is a piece of the slate rock on which Roger Williams landed when he came here in 1636 to hold forth his lively experiment of independence with strength and courage. May his spirit live in Brown men."

---

[4]: Martha Mitchell's Encyclopedia Brunoniana.

For 65 years the bear stood guard in front of Marvel Gymnasium but when the gym was closed in 1989 Bruno was moved to the College Green between Faunce House and Solomon Center and rededicated to Alma Mater and to the men and woman of Brown.

THE KODIAK BEAR

The Kodiak Bear – This giant was shot by Jack Durrell in 1938 on the Sitka Peninsula. Purchased and donated by Ronald M. Kimball, this 1,600 pound fighting bear has been a fixture at the University since its dedication on October 15, 1948. (Photo by Heather Caranci)

Not all of the university's bears are made of bronze. On October 15, 1948, the alumni of the mid west donated a stuffed bear to Brown after Ronald M. Kimball (1918) convinced his friend Jack Durrell, the big game hunter that shot the bear, to sell it.

Durrell and his guide came upon the bear on a morning in March 1938 on the Sitka Peninsula. The bear fought off four other bears before chasing a fifth over the top of the range. Durrell, who witnessed the bear's adventure, came upon him again after several hours and later described what happened next. He pumped three shots into the bear knocking him down with each direct hit, but after each shooting the bear rebounded and stood eventually charging toward the hunters. When the bear was finally much too close for comfort, Durrell fired a fourth and final shot into the bear and "...blasted him off the ridge into an alder-filled gulch..."[5] The approximately 1,600 pound fighting bear finally succumbed.

After Kimball's intervention, the bear was skinned and stuffed and housed in the trophy room in Brown's Faunce House for students and visitors alike to admire. Kodiak Bear has since been moved to the lobby of the new Meehan Auditorium where he stands today a proud symbol of Brown University strength.

---

[5] Martha Mitchell's Encyclopedia Brunoniana

THE MADDOCK ALUMNI CENTER BEAR

The Maddock Alumni Center Bear – The University dedicated it most unique bear statue on November 12, 1988. Inside this bronze bear mascot suit replica is a second bronze statue, that of a person wearing the suit, which can be seen by glimpsing into the bear's slightly open mouth. (Photo by Paul Caranci)

In the yard of Maddock Alumni Center on the university's campus stands a most unique five foot, six inch bronze casting of a bear. This impressionist bear was commissioned by the class of 1949 as a means of honoring outgoing university President Howard Swearer and gifted to the university. President Swearer's son Nicholas is the sculptor that was awarded the design work. On November 12, 1988 a dedication ceremony was held at which time a miniature replica measuring eighteen inches in height was presented to President Swearer.

What makes this bear statue so unique among the many others adorning the Brown campus is that this one is actually a bronze statue of a person wearing a bear suit. When viewing the bear through its open mouth, an observant spectator can make out a bronze "person" standing inside.

INDOMITABLE

A crane was needed to hoist this 10' bear known as Indomitable into place. British wildlife sculptor Nick Bibby explained the extraordinary process used in the creation of one of the Universities most recent additions. It was dedicated on November 2, 2013. (Photo by Heather Caranci)

Standing at the entrance of the Nelson Fitness Center in the Ittleson Quadrangle is yet another life-size male Kodiak bear. Indomitable replaces Bruno which was relocated when Marvel Gym closed in 1989 and is the work of renowned British wildlife sculptor Nick Bibby. The standing 10' bronze bear was commissioned by Brown's Public Art Committee and paid for with Percent-for-Art program funds in a desire to bring a bear back to the athletic complex. The Percent-for-Art fund devotes one percent of the budget for all new buildings and major renovations for campus art displays. Additional funding support for Indomitable was provided by Jonathan M. Nelson and H. Anthony Ittleson.

The two-hour installation took place with the use of a crane on the morning of Monday October 28, 2013. The statue was dedicated in appropriate ceremony on Saturday November 2nd concluding what was an eighteen-month process from inception to dedication. The prior Thursday, Bibby, who is known for his lifelike portrayals of animals, delivered a public lecture about the "tremendously complex" process he used in creating the statue. "The bear was fashioned using a new version of the old lost-wax method of casting that involved the initial creation of a one-fifth maquette that was then scanned, digitally enlarged and then printed in urethane foam, which provided the core of the final piece."

The bronze was cast in Gloucestershire, England at the renowned Pangolin Editions foundry. The finished product was crated and shipped by boat to the United States.

CESAR AUGUSTO

Cesar Augusto was arguably one of Rome's finest emperors. This bronze of Augustus lost its right arm during the hurricane of 1938. The presentation of this gift of 1854 graduate Moses Brown Ives Goddard was made to the University following chapel service on the first day of the academic year in 1906. (Photo by Heather Caranci)

• • •

Born Gaius Octavius on September 23, 63 BC, this future emperor was the son of a wealthy and politically powerful family that hailed from Velletri, Italy. Following the death of his father when young Octavius was just four, his mother remarried. Her new husband was uninterested in Octavius who was instead raised by his grandmother who just happened to be the sister of Julius Caesar. After her death in about 52 BC, his mother and stepfather took a more active part in raising him.

Following the assassination of Julius Caesar on the Ides of March in 44 BC, Octavius learned the contents of Caesar's will and at once determined that he would become his political successor as well as beneficiary to two-thirds of his estate. To his good fortune, Caesar had no living legitimate children and had adopted Octavius as his son and main heir. At this time Octavius took the name Gaius Julius Caesar, but in 27 BC, changed his name to Augustus. Some of his early decisions regarding the use of Caesar's money caused conflict with Mark Antony, one of Caesar's supporters. Those early conflicts seemed resolved when in October of 43BC, Octavian, Antony and a third leading Caesarian, Marcus Aemilius Lepidus, formed the Second Triumvirate. The Republic was divided among the three and each ruled as a military dictator. Within five years this union would dissolve because of their competing ambitions. Antony engaged Augustus in a losing effort in the Battle of Actium in 31 BC after which Antony committed suicide. Lepidus was eventually stripped of his power and driven into exile. Augustus continued to rule the entire Republic as a military dictator. He rejected traditional titles and called himself "Princeps Civitatis" or "First Citizen." The "Principate," his new constitutional framework, formed the first phase of the Roman Empire.

Augustus's reign was comparatively peaceful, at least in terms of large-scale conflicts, and eventually became known as "Pax Romana" or "The Roman Peace." During his reign he enlarged the empire and secured it with a buffer region of client states. He engaged a diplomatic peace with the Parthians, reformed the tax system, developed a network of roads connected with an official courier system, established a standing army and a Praetorian Guard, created Rome's first official police and fire fighting services and rebuilt much of the city.

Augustus died at age 75 on August 19, 14 AD after a short illness which may have been at the hands of his wife who some think poisoned him. He is remembered today as Rome's first and perhaps greatest emperor.

Imaginably that is the reason that 1854 graduate Moses Brown Ives Goddard chose to honor Augustus with a bronze statue that he gifted the University on September 19, 1906. Goddard made the presentation following chapel exercises on the first day of the academic year. He commissioned the sculpture to be an exact replica of the Augustus of Prima Porta statue currently located at the Vatican Museum in Rome, Italy. The original is one of the most iconic pieces of classical art as it embodies Greek sculptural traditions.

The Brown version is a painted bronze cast at the Nelli Foundry in Rome and depicts the life-sized Augustus standing in half stride. His right arm, which has essentially been missing ever since it was damaged in the great Hurricane of 1938, was in an upraised position. He is clothed in a decorated Roman military uniform and toga, traditional garb of the period. His left arm is draped with extra toga fabric and originally held a staff that, like the right arm, is now missing. A "genie" figure on a dolphin rests by his right leg.

Originally located on the Main Green in front of Rhode Island Hall in 1906, the statue was moved to its present location in front of the Sharpe Refectory in Wriston Quadrangle in September of 1952.

The move caused quite a stir among the students however as was illustrated by an editorial in the Brown Daily Herald in which the writer noted "…that his [Augustus] presence among Georgian Colonial architecture is one that 'Caesar, the aesthete, would abhor.'"[6]

---

[6] the Brown Daily Herald, October 27, 1952

MARCUS AURELIUS

This life-size equestrian bronze is one of the most aesthetically impressive statues in all of Providence. Like the statue of Caesar Augusto before it, a 1980 plan to move the statue of Marcus Aurelius to a different spot on the campus created quite a stir among students and faculty alike resulting in a petition of opposition signed by over 1,000 people. (Photo by Heather Caranci)

As you walk the Brown University campus along the western end of Simmons Quadrangle (formerly known as Lincoln Field) past the rear of Sayles Hall facing Thayer Street through the Soldiers Memorial Gate you will pass one of the most aesthetically impressive statues in the entire City of Providence – the Marcus Aurelius life-size equestrian bronze.

Born into a wealthy and politically prominent family in Italy on April 26, 121, Marcus Aurelius grew to be a dedicated student. Though he studied both Latin and Greek, it was the study of Stoics, such as the former slave Epictetus, whose philosophy emphasized fate, reason and self-restraint, that provided his greatest intellectual stimulation.

In the year 140, Aurelius was chosen to lead the senate. There he continued his study of philosophy and became interested in law. Just five years later he married Faustina, the daughter of emperor Antoninus, and over the years the couple had several children not all of whom survived to adulthood. His was a steady rise to power from that point and he became Emperor upon the death of his adopted father in 161. He was now known officially by this time as Marcus Aurelius Antoninus Augustus. Unlike the reign of his predecessor Antoninus, however, the reign of Aurelius was marked by war and disease. A war with the Parthian empire was waged over control of lands in the East and though successful, the soldiers returned to Rome carrying a disease that took years to eradicate killing a significant number of people in the interim. Shortly after the conclusion of the Parthian War, Rome was attacked by the Germans that crossed the Danube River. Aurelius's brother and co-leader Versus was killed in that battle leaving Aurelius to drive back the Germans on his own.

In 175 Aurelius had his authority challenged by Avidius Cassius who claimed the title of emperor after hearing that Aurelius was gravely ill. Aurelius was forced to take to flight once again, but Cassius was killed by his own soldiers before Aurelius could confront him. Instead of engaging in battle, Aurelius and Faustina toured the eastern provinces, but during this tour, Faustina suffered a fatal illness.

Aurelius died on March 17, 180 leaving his son Commodus to lead the Roman Empire. Despite the unsettling nature of his reign,

Aurelius is best remembered "for his contemplative nature and his rule driven by reason. A collection of his thoughts have been published in a work called *The Meditations*. Based on his Stoic beliefs, the work is filled with notes on life."[7]

Like the statue of Augustus Caesar, this beautiful equestrian that graces the Brown campus was a gift of 1854 graduate Moses Brown Ives Goddard who commissioned Hoppin and Field to create an exact replica of the original now housed in the Capitoline Museum at Rome. The original was more than likely cast during the 2nd century reign of Marcus Aurelius and remains the only bronze equestrian statue from ancient times still in existence today. Unfortunately Goddard didn't live long enough to see the work unveiled. That honor went to his brother Col. Robert Hale Ives Goddard, class of 1858, who dedicated the statue on June 1, 1908 following an impressive dissertation by Professor Walter Goodnow Everett on the philosophy of Marcus Aurelius.

The life-size bronze statue features a bearded Marcus Aurelius dressed in classical Roman garb that includes a tunic, cape and sandals. His right arm is outstretched with open hand, palm facing down. The emperor sits on a horse adorned with period military saddle, the right front leg lifted gracefully as if in a parade prance. The base is marble or limestone resting on a granite platform. This copy was cast in Rome at the Nelli Foundry.

In the 1980s, when a plan was proposed to develop the green space on which the statue now sits, the student body responded with a petition of over 1,000 signatures opposing the plan, a movement supported by faculty and staff alike. A further indication of the esteem with which the student body holds this iconic figure, was demonstrated in 1991 when the statue was abruptly removed to allow for much needed maintenance to the base. A bewildered student reporter crafted a front page headline in the Brown Daily Herald that proclaimed simply, "Marcus Aurelius Gone from Lincoln Field."

---

[7] "Marcus Aurelius," The Biography.com website, http://www.biography.com/people/marcus-aurelius-9192657

DANTE

This bronze bust of Dante, the esteemed author of the Divine Comedy, was sculpted by Paolo I. Abbate after the State's Italian community commissioned the work to commemorate the 600th *anniversary of Dante's death. (Photo by Heather Caranci)*

The Middle Ages Italian poet known simply as Dante was born Durante degli Alighier in Florence, Italy circa 1265 to a family presumed to be of some prestige. The family apparently had some loyalties to a political alliance known as the Guelphs, and were supportive of the Pope of Rome. It is also presumed that Dante was home schooled or educated in a chapter school generally attached to a church or monastery in Florence. Regardless of place, it is clear that he studied Tuscan poetry and admired the works of the poet Guido Guinizelli. He eventually discovered the Provencal poetry of the Troubadours and was influenced by Latin writers such as Cicero, Ovid and Virgil.

He claims to have fallen in love with Beatrice Portinari at the age of nine effectually setting an example of courtly love developed

centuries earlier in French and Provencal poetry and his love for Beatrice would ultimately become his reason for poetry and life. She appears in many of his works as quasi-divine, watching over him and
providing spiritual instruction. Her death in 1290 caused Dante to seek
refuge first in Latin literature and later in the study of philosophy at
religious schools including the Dominican Santa Maria Novella.

Dante was enmeshed in the Guelph-Ghibelline conflict
fighting for the Florentine Guelphs against the Ghibellines of Arezzo.
While he chose the right side, the success of the Guelphs was short
live, however as they soon splintered into the Black Guelphs who supported the Pope and the White Guelphs that craved greater independence from Rome in Flourentine affairs. Dante joined with the Whites,
but despite his political alliance, seemed favored by Pope Boniface
who dismissed all but Dante from a group of delegates sent by the
city's government to ascertain the Pope's intentions regarding a meeting with Charles of Valois, a brother of King Philip IV of France.
While Dante was still with the Pope, Charles of Valois entered Florence with the Black Guelphs destroying the largest part of the city and
killing several of their enemies. Dante was exiled for two years and
fined, a payment which he refused to make. The result was his permanent exile with the possibility of being burned at the stake if he returned without payment.

Although Dante initially tried to help the White Guelphs re-
gain power, he eventually became disenchanted and withdrew from
politics. For him, exile was a form of death as he believed it stripped
him of much of his identity and heritage. Throughout this time and
most of his life Dante continued to write. Convivio (The Banquet),
Monarchia, La Vita Nuova (The New Life) and De vulgari Eloquentia
(On the Eloquence of Vernacular) are within his portfolio of great
works, but it is the Divine Comedy that ranks among his greatest. This
book describes Dante's journey through Hell, Purgatory and Paradise,
guided first by Virgil, the Roman poet, and then by Beatrice, his first
love.

Dante contracted malaria while returning to Ravenna from a
diplomatic mission to Venice and died at the age of 56 in 1321. He is
buried at the Church of San Pier Maggiore in Ravenna in a tomb
erected for him in 1483. Though Florence eventually regretted his exile and tried to reclaim his body, Revenna refused to give up the

remains. Florence erected a tomb in his honor called the Cenotaph in Basilica of Santa Croce, but it has remained empty all these years. On the front of that tomb is inscribed the words Onorate L'atissimo poeta which translates, "Honor the most exhalted poet."

In 1921, celebrating the 600th anniversary of Dante's death, the State's Italian community commissioned Paolo I. Abbate to create a bust of the great poet and presented it to Brown University on December 9th in impressive ceremony. Set on a granite plinth and located on Prospect Street in front of the John Hay Library, the larger than life bust depicts Dante wearing a cap and a laurel wreath of a poet. The inscription on the granite pedestal proclaims the bust a gift of the Rhode Island Italians to Brown University in commemoration of the sixth centenary of Dante's death. In August of 1921 the Rhode Island Grand Lodge of the Sons of Italy established four scholarships at Brown. These "Dante" scholarships were awarded to Brown students who made good progress in the study of the Italian language.

RECLINING FIGURE NO. 2 - BRIDGE-PROP 1963

Reclining Figure No. 2, also known as Bridge Prop 1963 and 3 Piece Reclining Figure is the only example of Henry Moore's work in Providence. Described as a "female figure cast in bronze" by Brunoniana Encyclopedia, it weighs in a over a ton and is one of an edition of six pieces. (Photo by Heather Caranci)

Alternately known as *Reclining Figure No. 2*, *Bridge Prop* and *Three Piece Reclining Figure*, the Bridge Prop may have more monikers than any other monument in Providence. According to its sculptor, Henry Moore, the sculpture was inspired by London's Waterloo Bridge in which one part of the bridge rests against another – thus providing the subtitle Bridge Prop. The work consists of three rounded and arched abstract shapes resting on a rectangular base and was cast in Berlin, Germany in 1963 by Hermann Noack Bildgiesseri.

Moore noted that it is actually "an exploration of the body through the interconnectedness of its various bifurcated pieces."[8]

---

[8]http://brown.edu/about/public-art/gifts/henry-more-reclining-figure-no-2-bridge-prop-1963

Located near the Faunce House on the College Green, the work was a gift from Mr. and Mrs. David Finn of New Rochelle, New York, the parents of three Brown students, and was given to the University in 1974. It has since become a fixture on the Brown campus, one that is frequently climbed upon and photographed. Martha Mitchell's Encyclopedia Brunoniana describes the sculpture as a "female figure cast in bronze." Weighing over a ton, it is actually in three parts, the first leaning against the second and the third free standing.

The Finns, who were close friends of Henry Moore and his family, photographed Bridge Prop from many angles and then collaborated with poet Donald Hall in the publication of *As The Eye Moves...A Sculpture by Henry Moore*. The book "focuses on the sculpture and the experience of space around it."[9]

Moore is a renowned 20th century British sculptor whose work appears on Ivy League campuses around the country. This is the only example of Moore's work in Providence and is one of an edition of six.

---

[9]http://brown.edu/about/public-art/gifts/henry-more-reclining-figure-no-2-bridge-prop-1963

GROUP OF THREE, THE PEMBROKE

Group of Three, The Pembroke – Brown professor Hugh Townley sculpted this work for the Class of 1965 and, after a "cool reception" that resulted in a four-year delay, it was installed on campus in 1969. (Photo by Heather Caranci)

The Pembroke class of 1965 commissioned Brown University professor emeritus and renowned sculptor Hugh Townley to create an artwork that could be placed on campus as a permanent addition to the Universities prized compositions. Townley, who taught at Brown for many years, is known for powerful formal sculptures that communicate through a personal vocabulary of forms that emerged over his forty year career.

The three large-scale concrete elements of this particular work were installed in 1969. The pieces spell "ART" in the abstract. The three monoliths are grouped together on one base, also made of concrete, although the original design had the three pieces popping up from the ground with no base. Robert Freeman and Vivienne Lasky point out in their impressive book, *Hidden Treasures: Public Sculpture in Providence,* that the design changes, as well as the four year delay in "erecting the sculpture, are indicative of the cool reception frequently generated by contemporary works."

This sculpture is one of an edition of two pieces. The second piece is located in Lincoln, Massachusetts at the DeCordova Museum.

ONE AND ONE HALF (1 ½)

This bronze and steel sculpture known as One and One Half (1½) is the 1984 composition of Carla Lavatelli and was gifted to the University by Artemis Joukowsky and his wife Martha. (Photo by Paul Caranci)

A second abstract on the Brown campus, "1 ½" consists of two large disks in parallel formation. One disc, made of bronze, is an almost full circle with circular cutouts of various sizes. The second disc is of steel construction, is more crescent in shape, and is also pierced with circular holes of various sizes. The two discs sit on a base of Swedish granite set near the entrance to the Universities Science Library.

Like America One, this sculpture was the gift of Artemis Joukowsky and his wife Martha. Dedicated on May 25, 1985 it is the 1984 composition of Carla Lavatelli.

S.75-AL-AMERICA ONE

S.75 –AL-America One - Is the work of award winning Yugoslavian artist Dusan Dzmonja and is made of small aluminum pieces forming a honeycomb surface on the six interlocking sections. (Photo by Paul Caranci)

Artemis Joukowsky, working with various members of Brown's administration and faculty, formed the "sculpture committee" in the mid-1980s for the purpose of determining the appropriateness of any donation of sculpture that might adorn the University's grounds. In October 1990, Joukowsky offered his own donation to Brown's collection of sculptured art. America One is the work of award winning Yugoslavian artist Dusan Dzmonja best known for the use of circles and spheres in his work, which most often used found metal to honor the heroes and victims of World War II.

America One is made of small aluminum pieces forming a honeycomb surface on the six interlocking sections that shape a sphere. It is located near the west entrance of the Thomas J. Watson Ctr. for Information Technology.

CIRCLE DANCE

Circle Dance – Though eleven figures can be counted in this sculpture by Tom Friedman, the original design included only ten figures. Prior to coming to its final resting place at Brown, the sculpture "danced" at Frieze Art Fair in London's Regent's Park. (Photo by Heather Caranci)

Drawing inspiration from the Henri Matisse painting *La Danse*, American artist Tom Friedman created Circle Dance, a life-size stainless steel sculpture that was anonymously gifted to Brown University. The sculpture depicts eleven life-size figures holding hands while dancing as if around an invisible maypole. The original design included only ten figures. It measures 22 feet in diameter and weighs 3,200 pounds. The installation, which began on November 26, 2012, took four days to complete.

Friedman art makes use of ordinary everyday materials. Circle Dance was initially crafted in maquette using aluminum foil oven roasting trays. A close inspection of the stainless steel cast reveals imprints of the word "bottom" and the pan's manufacturer.

• • •

Prior to coming to its final resting place at Brown, the sculpture "danced" at Frieze Art Fair in London's Regent's Park. According to the Stephen Friedman Gallery's website, "The figures are at once light-footed and unerringly enduring; frozen in time yet brought to life on their reflective surfaces."

CARRIE CLOCK TOWER

Carrie Clock Tower – The second of two Providence memorials to Carrie Brown Bajnotti, this impressive tower was the gift of Carrie's husband Paul and is the work of Guy Lowell who later designed the Boston Museum of Fine Arts. (Post card image from author's collection)

The story of Carrie Brown is actually a continuation of an intense story of the love between two sisters and between each sister and the man she married.

When Carrie Brown Bajnotti succumbed to the effects of pneumonia in Palermo, Sicily in 1892 at the age of 46, her husband Paul, an Italian Count and Foreign Affairs Officer, was "sorrowed and heartbroken." He commissioned two monuments to her memory to be erected in her hometown of Providence. The story of the first, the Bajnotti Fountain in Burnside Park, along with Paul and Carrie's moving love story can be found in Chapter 24 and should be read in conjunction with this one.

The Clock Tower is the second of her memorials constructed in Providence. It was built in 1904 and is at the corner of Prospect and

Waterman Streets located just within the wrought iron fence that demarcates the front campus of Brown University. Bajnotti conducted an extensive search for the perfect architect to design and oversee the construction of the tower and following a long competition, selected Guy Lowell. Lowell, as it turns out, was the absolute right choice. He first designed a most impressive tribute to Carrie and was later selected to design the Boston Museum of Fine Arts.

SLAVERY MEMORIAL

Brown's Slavery Memorial was dedicated on September 27, 2014 in acknowledgement of the state's early economic dependence on the slave trade and the role of the university's founders in the "Triangle Trade" of rum, slaves and molasses. The memorial is strategically located, next to Brown's oldest building, University Hall, which was constructed with the support of at least three slaves. (Photo by Heather Caranci)

Eight years in the making, the newest monument to grace the grounds of the Brown campus was dedicated on Saturday September 27, 2014, just as this book was nearing completion. The monument acknowledges Rhode Island's early economic dependence on the slave trade and the role of Brown University founders in the "Triangle Trade" of rum, slaves and molasses.

This impressive work by one of America's most accomplished contemporary sculptors, Martin Puryear, is comprised of three elements; two designed by Puryear and one the brainchild of Jo-Ann Conklin and the Brown Public Art Committee. The first element is a partially submerged giant ball and chain with the third link of the chain broken, symbolic of the end of slavery and celebrating the freedom guaranteed to all men by the Constitution; the second is a nearby cylindrical granite plaque inscribed with information acknowledging Brown University's 18th century connection to the trans-Atlantic slave trade; finally, the site itself becomes an element of the sculpture as it is located near University Hall. Built in 1770, University Hall is the oldest building on the campus and was constructed with the support of at least three slaves.

Chapter 2

Providence College

1 Cunningham Square

ST. MARTIN DE PORRES

Two statues of de Porres are on the campus

The son of a Spanish nobleman and a freed slave, St. Martin de Porres was originally rejected by the Dominican order because of his mixed race. During a life dedicated to the less fortunate witnesses reported that St. Martin could bi-locate and was lifted in the air when experiencing ecstasy during prayer. (Photo by Heather Caranci)

• • •

Sixteenth century Spanish nobleman Don Juan de Porres may not have loved Ana Velazquez, but the two did, at the very least, have an affair that resulted in the birth of Martin de Porres on December 9, 1579. In fact, after the birth of Martin's sister Juana two years later, Don Juan abandoned the family to a life of poverty. Being both poor and the illegitimate son of a freed slave of African or possibly Native American descent didn't make life easy for Martin. Though Ana tried to support her children by taking in laundry, she could not and Martin was sent to a primary school for two years. There he learned the medical arts through his placement with a barber (also a surgeon in those times.) Despite his hardships, or perhaps because of them, young Martin spent hours each night in prayer, and soon desired a life with a religious order. Such a life in 16th century Peru was not a privilege afforded to descendents of Africans or Indians however. Instead, fifteen year old de Porres asked the Dominicans of Holy Rosary Priory to allow him to serve them as a "donado," a volunteer that is allowed to live with the order and wear the habit in exchange for the performance of menial tasks around the monastery. To his delight, his offer was accepted and Martin was received as the order's servant boy.

Eventually Martin was allowed to resume his work in barbering and healing and performed many cures which may have been more miraculous than medical in nature. Despite the legendary status that he was developing he continued in the performance of more menial work in the kitchen and laundry of the monastery.

By the year 1602, Martin's work, especially his "healing" work, was becoming noticed and the Dominican Prior decided to allow Martin to take the vows of the order despite the Peruvian law prohibiting such. Among the Order's 300 members were some that didn't share the Prior's enthusiasm toward Martin and they objected to his overture. Martin was rejected for membership and subjected to ridicule as "illegitimate," a "mulatto dog," and a "descendant of slaves." The following year, Martin was allowed to profess religious vows, but only as a Dominican lay brother, a status he initially rejected. Still, he remained faithful to the Order and when his convent was in debt, offered himself for sale as a slave to help satisfy the debt.

· · ·

St. Martin de Porres – Fr. Thomas McGlynn actually designed two statues of St. Martin. This smaller version appears in a serene water setting in the McGlynn Sculpture Court outside Hunt-Cavanaugh Hall. (Photo by Heather Caranci)

Deeply devoted to the Blessed Sacrament, he was in prayer one night when the step on which he was kneeling caught fire. Perhaps in a state of ecstasy, Martin ignored the chaos that followed and remained kneeling in prayer untouched by the flames.

At age 34 and now wearing the habit of a lay brother, Martin worked the infirmary where he would remain until his death twenty-five years later. In his care for the sick, both inside and outside the convent, he displayed an unfailing patience and many miracles were attributed to him. He ministered to both Spanish nobles and African slaves. When he was admonished by one of his own for accepting the stretched-out hand of a near naked, aged and ulcerated beggar and giving him respite in Martin's bed, he responded, "Compassion, my dear Brother, is preferable to cleanliness." This sentiment governed his life.

During an epidemic that struck Lima, some sixty friars took ill and many were locked in a distant section of the convent for fear of

• • •

contagion. It is said that Martin "passed through locked doors to care for them, a phenomenon which was reported in the residence more than once." It was reported that he would appear suddenly beside someone without doors having been opened! After being forbidden to take in any more of the stricken for fear of further contagion, Martin convinced his sister to offer her house in the country for their lodging.

De Porres changed not only the hearts and minds of the poor and sick but of the "enlightened" as well. On one occasion Martin came upon an Indian dying in the street from a dagger wound. Unable to transport the injured man to his sister's house, he carried him back to his own room at the convent. The Prior reprimanded Martin for his disobedience and Martin offered in reply, "Forgive my error, and please instruct me, for I did not know that the precept of obedience took precedence over that of charity." From that point forward, the Prior allowed Martin to follow his instincts in the exercise of mercy.

Martin found time to beg for the money necessary to feed up to 160 indigents a day as he continued his work in the kitchen, laundry and infirmary and was blessed with many gifts of the Holy Spirit. It was reported that light filled a room where he prayed. He could bi-locate and was lifted in the air when experiencing ecstasy during prayer. He possessed miraculous knowledge and was credited with instantaneous cures. Some report that he could even communicate with the animals.

Word of his miracles spread so by the time of his death on November 3, 1639, de Porres was respected by many of the Dominicans and lay people of Peru. The miracles and graces received by those that invoked his name increased so dramatically after his death that in 1664, after laying in the grave for 25 years, Martin's body was exhumed and found to be "intact and exhaling a fine fragrance."

In 1763 Pope Clement XIII issued a decree affirming Martin's heroism and he was beatified by Pope Gregory XVI in 1837. He was elevated to sainthood in Rome by Pope John XXIII on May 6, 1962. He is commemorated worldwide in films, statuary, portraiture and by schools and medical buildings that bear his name.

As is typical of his icons, this statue of St. Martin de Porres depicts him both at prayer with his right hand clutching a cross, and at work, holding a broom with his left. The larger-than-life bronze was cast at the Mariani Foundry in Pietrasanta, Italy, and unlike an earlier cast, is free standing. The statue rests on a base of concrete. The traditional animals that adorn de Porres' feet are absent from this cast. Designed by the late Dominican Friar and former member of the Providence College faculty, Thomas McGlynn, the statue was cast in 1958 and dedicated on the campus on November 3, 1979. McGlynn is the artist responsible for several of the statues on the Providence College campus including a smaller statue of St. Martin that is at the McGlynn Sculpture Court outside Hunt-Cavanaugh Hall.

ST. DOMINIC De GUZMAN

St. Domenic de Guzman died in 1221 never achieving his goal of martyrdom, but founded the order of priests and nuns bearing his name. The Dominican Friars teach at Providence College and at many other colleges and universities throughout the United States. (Photo by Heather Caranci)

He was described by his friend, Blessed Cecilia Ceasarini, as "handsome and somewhat fair" with a full head of reddish hair and beard. His beautiful eyes "shown a sort of radiance which drew everyone to respect and love him." Excepting when he was moved to compassion at the sight of someone's troubles, he was cheerful and alert.

Dominic de Guzman was born between 1771 and 1773 to Spanish nobleman Felix de Guzman and his wife Joan, a woman of unusual sanctity herself regarded by locals as a saint. From his earliest days he was prepared for a religious life and made education and charity the centerpieces of his life. In fact, his most treasured youthful possession, a collection of religious books inscribed on parchment, was sold so he could give the money to the poor. "I could not bear to prize dead skins," he would later say, "when living skins were starving and in need."

At age 25, while still a student, he was ordained and lived under the strict rule of St. Augustine. This discipline is something he taught to others throughout his life. He was soon made a sub-prior, then prior when Diego d'Azevado was made Bishop of Osma.

Following appointment as canon of the cathedral by Martin de Bazan of Osma Dominic was asked to travel with the Bishop on a diplomatic mission that crossed into the south of France. It was there that they encountered the Albigenses. This band of educated heretics denied the doctrine of the Trinity and believed in a dual creator; a good creator of the invisible and a bad creator of the material world whom they called a murderer and a liar. They regarded the Old Testament as the bible of the devil and believed that all the patriarchs and prophets were damned. Christ, they contended, was a wicked man but they reserved their most virulent hatred for John the Baptist who they regarded as one of the greatest demons. They rejected all the sacraments, especially marriage, and believed that once they received the "Consolamentum" they were made perfect and were free to commit suicide, something they did with frequency.

The host of the inn where Dominic and the Bishop lodged was an Albigensian and Dominic spent the entire night talking to him. By morning, he had converted the man who renounced his former ways. Despite the continuation of the movement, the experience changed

Dominic's life and convinced him that God required him to spend the rest of his life teaching in the world.

It was in his work as a teacher that the first miracle associated with Dominic took place. In the City of Fanjeaux Dominic was challenged to a formal debate with the Albigenses where he was bestowed the honor of defending the Faith against its adversaries. Though presenting a case that resulted in the complete embarrassment of the heretical champion, fear of the heretics they lived among prevented the umpires from rendering the obvious verdict. Instead, they called for a "trial by fire" to be the final arbiter. First the heretic tossed his debate papers into the fire where they were immediately consumed by the flames. Then Dominic threw his defense into the fire. Not only were they not burned, but they were immediately cast back. Dominic tossed the papers into the flame a second and third time, but to the continued amazement of the crowd, the result remained constant thereby leaving no doubt as to the divine character of the truth contained therein. Yet, despite the miraculous turn of events, the Albigenses remained undeterred in their heresy.

The Albigenses continued to preach their heresy and gained many converts. Young Catholic girls were not only exposed to the wrong examples in their homes, they were sometimes sent to Albidensian convents to be educated. Dominic, acting on visions, established convents for girls who were converted from their heresy and established homes for his preaching friars who were subjected to "a strict rule of poverty, study and prayer."

Following the 1208 murder of his papal legate, the personal representative of the Pope to foreign nations, Pope Innocent transitioned from prayer to military force to suppress the heresy. Rather than participate in the civil war, Dominic continued to preach. Many attempts were made on his life and when asked what he would do if captured by the Albigenses, he said, "I would tell them to kill me slowly and painfully, a little at a time, so that I might have a more glorious crown in Heaven."

Dominic also had no part in the Episcopal courts of the Inquisition established in southern France to work with civil authorities nor did he approve of the executions it ordered. In fact, Dominic is alleged to have saved the life of a condemned man by insisting that if released, he would die a good Catholic, a prophesy that

• • •

was fulfilled years later when the man entered the Dominican Order. He always insisted that prayer rather than violence would be the key to overcoming the enemies of the faith, saying "Arm yourself with prayer instead of a sword; be clothed with humility instead of fine raiment."

Dominic spent nearly ten years preaching hoping over that time to enlighten preachers with zeal and spirit with which to spread the message. The concept of someone other than a priest preaching, however, was a new one and was met with some hesitation. Dominic was persistent and eventually won the approval of Bishop Foulques who in 1014 consented to a new order which eventually gained the verbal support of Pope Innocent III.

A meeting was held at Prouille in August 1016 to plan the Order. It was attended by 17 men who resorted to prayer to choose a constitution dedicated to the rule of St. Augustine. Following the death of Innocent III, Pope Honorius III formally confirmed the Order and its constitutions declaring the brothers "the champions of the faith and the true lights of the world."

The Friar Preachers, popularly known as the Dominicans, first met at Prouille with Dominic urging them on methods of preaching and continuous study and training. The remainder of Dominic's life was spent developing the new Order. The Pope provided the church of St. Sixtus in Rome to be used as the official center of Dominican activities. He continued to preach and perform miracles.

One account tells of a woman named Gutadona who, after hearing Domenic preach, returned home only to find her son dead. She took him from his cradle and carried him to Dominic who prayed fervently, made the sign of the cross, and raised the lifeless child.

Dominic died in 1221 never achieving his goal of martyrdom. Instead the ministry of the Word became the primary goal of his new Order. During the last few years of his life Dominic preached from the heart rather than from the book and always preached love. By the time of his death Orders were established in Poland, Scandinavia and Palestine and monasteries in Canterbury, London and Oxford.

Today the Order is worldwide and noted for its intellectual achievement. It has become the agent of scholastic theology and philosophy presiding over a number of religious institutions including Providence College.

The life-size bronze of Saint Dominic stands in front the house of the President of Providence College, founded and staffed by the Order he founded. In statue Dominic has a tonsured head and beard. He wears a flowing cassock, holds a book in his left hand and leans forward in purposeful stride seemingly unaffected by thorny wood on which he walks.

The first cast of this statue, sculpted by Thomas McGlynn in 1974, is located in the Dominican Church of the Madonna dell Arco in Naples, Italy. The Providence College cast, done in 1978, is set on a simple concrete cube and was dedicated in 1978 to the memory of the Providence College girls who died in a Christmas-time dormitory fire the year prior.

VERITAS ETERNALITER JUVENIS
aka Mr. & Mrs. Slavin

Translating "Truth is Always Young," Veritas Eternaliter Juvenis depicts a man and a woman who walks from the cloak that represents school and family. The shedding of the cloak symbolizes the young couple's transition from the security of home and school to their venture into the world. (Photo by Heather Caranci)

• • •

In 1974, Joseph "Bo" and Alice Bernstein gifted this statue to Providence College. Commissioned a year earlier and designed by noted artist Gilbert Franklin, the life-size bronze depicts a man and a woman in stride. The man's right hand affectionately holds the woman's left and the two hands hang waist high in front of them. The couple's other arms lock in a half-embrace as they appear in conversation.

The woman wears a long gown and the cloak worn by the male figure seems to encircle both of them though they appear to be emerging from it. The cloak represents home, school and family, and leaving it signifies their departure from that foundation and their entry into the world. The statue itself, which represents the spirit of youth and coeducation, stands on a base of concrete.

The Latin title, "Veritas Eternaliter Juvenis," translates, "Truth is Always Young." The statue is located outside Slavin Center and was dedicated at the 1974 commencement ceremonies of the college's first co-educational class. Prior to September 1969 and dating back to the inaugural class of September 1919, Providence College was an all-male institution.

ST. THOMAS AQUINAS

Thomas Aquinas – The Dominican Friars of Providence College welcomed the newest statue dedicated on campus on August 27, 2013. The 800 pound bronze of the Angelic Doctor, arguably the greatest theologian, was designed by Sylvia Nicolas and cast at a foundry in Utah. (Photo by Heather Carauci)

• • •

Thomas Aquinas was born in Roccasecca, Italy in late 1226, the son of Count Landulph of Aquino. When Thomas was just five years old, his father placed him in the care of the Benedictines of Monte Casino where he surpassed all the other pupils in both knowledge and virtue. As soon as he was of age to choose a profession, Thomas stunned his family by declaring his intentions to renounce the world and enter the Order of St. Dominic. His family tried with desperation over the ensuing years to change his mind, but Thomas prevailed and joined the Order in 1243 at the age of seventeen.

He studied in Cologne under St. Albert the Great where, though brilliant, he was nicknamed the "dumb ox." The moniker had nothing to do with his intelligence, but rather was reflective of his mute-like demeanor and very large size. At age twenty-two he published his first works and at the age of thirty-one, received his doctorate.

Thomas was called to Rome by Pope Urban IV and was appointed to a teaching position. There, Thomas wrote vociferously (his writings filled twenty immense volumes) and preached with extraordinary results, but persistently refused any ecclesiastical distinction. In 1274, while on his way to the second Council of Lyons, Thomas became ill. He died at the Cistercian monastery leaving his greatest work, the Summa Theologica, still unfinished. Thomas Aquinas is widely considered to be one of the most influential, perhaps the greatest, theologians of all time." On July 18, 1323, just fifty years after his death, Pope John XXII made Thomas a saint. St. Thomas was further honored by the Catholic Church when in 1567 Pope Pius V declared Thomas Aquinas the fifth Latin Doctor of the Church and commissioned the first edition of Aquinas' *opera omnia*, often called the *editio Piana* in honor of the Pope.

On August 27, 2013, the Dominican Friars of Providence College welcomed the newest statue dedicated on campus. The Angelic Doctor was delivered by pick-up truck and seven men carried the 800 pound bronze to the outside of the newly opened Ruane Center for the Humanities where it was hoisted onto two-tiered granite blocks outside the passageway that links the Ruane Center with the Phillips Memorial Library. Sculpted in clay by Sylvia Nicolas of Mount Vernon, New Hampshire, and cast in bronze at a foundry in Utah, the four feet high statue depicts St. Thomas Aquinas in a sitting position. His right hand holds an open book that rests on his right thigh. His left hand is raised inviting people to the truth. The sunburst shield, Thomas's symbol, is emblazoned on his chest and is sculpted on the passageway above him along with a Dominican shield on either side.

POPE JOHN XXIII

Pope John XXIII – Canonized a Catholic Saint on April 27, 2014 by Pope Francis, the man born Angelo Giusseppe Roncalli is memorialized in a bronze bust sculpted by Providence College's Fr. Thomas McGlynn and dedicated on campus on October 2, 1993 (Photo by Heather Caranci)

Pope John XXIII was born Angelo Giusseppe Roncalli in November 1881, the third of thirteen surviving children. He was the first born son of a poor farming family in Scotto Il Monte, Italy, He always remained very proud of his humble roots and this perhaps is the reason for one of his most extraordinary characteristics throughout life; his "ordinariness."

In 1904 the future Pope was ordained into the Franciscan Order and studied cannon law in Rome. There he worked as the Bishop's secretary, taught church history at the seminary and was the publisher of the diocesan paper.

He learned of the horrors of war through his participation in World War I as a stretcher-bearer and chaplain in the Italian army. In 1921 he was appointed the national director for the Propagation of the Faith and in1925 was named a papal diplomat serving at various times in Bulgaria, Turkey, Greece and France. While serving in this capacity in Turkey and Greece during World War II, now Archbishop Roncalli saved the lives of several Jews fleeing the Holocaust. He provided them with transit visas and other documentation that allowed them to leave Europe. For that he was honored as one of the "Righteous Among Nations," a recognition of non-Jews who risked their lives to save Jews.

In 1953 Roncalli was named a Cardinal and appointed patriarch of Venice. On October 28, 1958, he was elected the 262nd Roman Catholic Pope taking the name John after his father and St. John Lateran, one of two patrons of Rome's cathedral.

Known for his proverbial wit, John met with many world political leaders during his papal reign. During the 1962 Cuban Missile Crisis, as Russia and the United States teetered on the brink of nuclear war, John broadcast a message on Vatican Radio urging a peaceful resolution to the crisis. Kremlin officials heard the message and informed Nikita Khrushchev who agreed to be "the man of peace." Within days, Khrushchev began withdrawing missiles from the island of Cuba, thereby defusing the crisis.

Pope John wrote several encyclicals including "Pacem in Terris" or "Peace on Earth" in which he called for the world's populations to coexist in harmony. He increased the membership in the College of Cardinals and set the tone of Vatican II by pronouncing his intentions to make use of "the medicine of mercy rather than that of severity."

• • •

Pope John XXIII died on June 3, 1963. On his deathbed he explained his papal actions saying, "It is not that the gospel has changed; it is that we have begun to understand it better. Those who have lived as long as I have... were enabled to compare different cultures and traditions, and know that the moment has come to discern the signs of the times, to seize the opportunity and to look far ahead."

The very popular Pope was beatified in 2000 by St. Pope John Paul II and, despite having only one miracle to his credit, was canonized a Catholic Saint on April 27, 2014 by Pope Francis.

The bronze bust of Pope John XXIII is another work of Dominican Friar Thomas McGlynn. It was originally intended as the head study for a proposed nine foot statue of the Pope to be installed as a monument in Italy. Though the monument was never commissioned, the bust was twice cast in bronze. The first cast is at the Bishop's Conference in Rome. This statue represents the second casting. It was installed in the McGlynn Sculpture Court at Providence College in the summer of 1992 and was dedicated on October 2, 1993. The twice-life size bust depicts the Pontiff wearing typical papal vestments and rests on a base of polished granite.

THE GROTTO AT ST. DOMINIC CHAPEL

The Grotto at St. Domenic Chapel – The Grotto, a smaller version of the original, was constructed using some of the material that was salvaged when the original Grotto was dismantled. The original marble statue of St. Domenic receiving the rosary from Our Lady remains the focal point. (Photo by Heather Caranci)

To honor the 69 graduates who gave their last full measure of devotion to the allied effort in World War II, Rev. Charles H. McKenna, OP, Chaplain of Providence College undertook the task of administering the construction of a memorial. The War Memorial Grotto of Our Lady of the Rosary was designed by Oliver O. Gauvin and built to completion by the Westcott Construction Company under the direction of Charles J. Fogarty in May, 1948. The project began the previous summer and was built of flagstone and fieldstone. Two white Carrara marble statues depicting Our Lady presenting a rosary to St. Dominic were placed in the alcove at the top of the stone Grotto. Two black granite slabs imported from Sweden were inscribed with the names of the deceased. The names of donors contributing $100 or

Detail of the two white Carrara marble statues depicting St. Domenic receiving the rosary from Our Lady. (Photo by Heather Caranci)

more to the $100,000 installation were inscribed on additional black granite plaques that were placed around the amphitheater. Bronze alter appointments and a Wurlitzer organ that could be removed to the indoors during inclement weather, completed to grotto memorial.

The memorial was dedicated on Mother's Day, May 9, 1948, before an audience of almost 10,000 which included church dignitaries, civic and political leaders. On June 6, 1948, just four days before its 30th commencement, the college celebrated the first Baccalaureate Mass at the Grotto.

Over the years several additions were made including the installation of fourteen bronze Stations of the Cross that were mounted on a retaining wall. Inclement weather forced the postponement of more than one Mass, however, and the site eventually became more recreational in nature acquiring the nickname of "Grotto Beach." The Grotto eventually fell into disrepair and a decision was made to build

• • •

Services and commencement exercises were frequently held in the War Memorial Grotto of Our Lady of the Rosary since its dedication on May 9, 1948. However, a decision was made to build a new chapel on the site, relocating a smaller version of the Grotto on the grounds near the 2001 construction. (Post card image from the author's collection)

a new chapel on the site with the essential components of the Grotto being relocated in or near the chapel.

St. Dominic's Chapel was dedicated on February 2, 2001 as the school's main chapel. There is a smaller Grotto on the side of the chapel built using some of the material salvaged from the original. Of course, the marble statue of St. Dominic receiving the rosary from Our Lady remains the focal point of the new grotto.

Chapter 3

Rhode Island College

600 Mount Pleasant Avenue

METAMORPHOSIS

The Metamorphosis is a series of five stones of different shapes and sizes, but all five are of equal volume and weight. The granite stones represent a student's growth during the college years. (Photo by Paul Caranci)

The five stones of the Metamorphosis are found in a semi-circular formation spread out in a 200' radius wrapping around RIC's Nazarian Performing Arts Center. (Photo by Paul Caranci)

To many casual observers Metamorphosis might simply blend into the landscape appearing as a series of unrelated decorative stones. Rather, this collection of five elipsoid granite stones, scattered in a 200' radius and wrapping around the courtyard of the Nazarian Performing Arts Center in an almost semi-circular formation, is the multi-pieced work of art of Jonathan Bonner.

The five stones vary in size and shape and are positioned sequentially from the shortest (measuring 2' high) to the tallest (measuring 8' in height). Perhaps the most intriguing feature of this sculpture is the fact that, despite the obvious size variations, each stone is of equal volume and weight.

According to sculptor Jonathan Bonner, who was commissioned by the Rhode Island Council on the Arts, the sculpture represents the growth a student goes through during their college career. Installed in 2000, the work is part of the college's permanent collection.

THE ANCHOR

The Anchor has been the enduring symbol of Rhode Island College since it was gifted to the school by the 1926 graduating class. Originally intended to promote school spirit, it was the object of student pranks and a statewide game of hide and seek. (Photo by Paul Caranci)

The anchor has long been associated with Rhode Island College. It is a mascot of sorts. Students and athletes are known as *Anchormen* and the schools newspaper is the called *The Anchor*. But there has not always been a physical manifestation of an anchor on campus. That was the brainchild and gift of the graduating class of 1926. Realizing that school spirit was lacking the student council believed that a competition might stimulate some much needed character. That's when it was determined that an anchor would be obtained and used as an award to draw the classes together with the class holding it responsible for its public display.

According to Dr. Mary Keefe, a member of the class of '28, the anchor was the perfect icon because it "symbolized the anchor in the state flag and our college's relationship to the State."[10] Over the ensuing years, the competition that began as a song contest, with the anchor being awarded to the class that composed and performed the best song on song night, morphed into "stunt night," a competition among classes to see which class could "steal" the anchor away from the class that held it. This variation of the tradition caused the class in possession of the prize to "hide" it from the other classes only to bring it out once a year – on stunt night. Initially the anchor had to be hidden on campus but later classes determined that since the college was a state entity, any state property was fair game for hiding the anchor. Rumor has it that one year the anchor was even "hidden" in the State House!

Getting the anchor became more of a game with each new class until it "became unpleasant and the classes generally felt getting it by work would mean more," according to Professor Marion Wright, a member of the class of 1944.[11] This, she argued, takes away the college pride that winning the anchor was meant to instill.

Today, the anchor can be observed pretty readily, for it is "hidden" in plain view on the Quad displayed like the monument it has become, just outside of the James P. Adams Library.

---

[10] The Anchor, November 17, 1959. Page 4
[11] The Anchor November 17, 1959. Page 4

UNTITLED
Cor-Ten steel sculpture #3

Untitled – (Cor-Ten Steel Sculpture #3) This work of RI School of Design Instructor Joseph Goto was once located in Kennedy Plaza in celebration of the 1ˢᵗ inauguration of Mayor Buddy Cianci. It was relocated to the RIC campus when Cianci decided to revamp Kennedy Plaza. RIC was forced to move it when construction began on the Alex and Ani building. It now sits in storage awaiting a new location on campus. (Photo by Paul Caranci)

• • •

This untitled work of art was created by Rhode Island School of Design Instructor Joseph Goto who started it in 1960 when he was still teaching at the University of Michigan. According to the sculptor, the four-ton piece reflects the tension, the "demented vitality," of the late sixties. Goto prefers his work untitled so the viewer can interpret it without trying to apply the artist's title to the interpretation.

Goto was the first to use jagged Cor-ten steel in sculpture. The original piece also contained stainless steel tubing for a sense of contrast to the texture and color, but the tubing was broken off in what can be described only as an abandonment of maintenance. In 1975 the sculpture was placed on Kennedy Plaza for the City's celebration of the new mayoral leadership of Vincent "Buddy" Cianci who was committed to the revitalization of the downtown area. In April 1984, however, when Cianci approved plans for the reconstruction of Kennedy Plaza, Providence decided it no longer had a use for the piece. That's when, according to Goto, he received a letter advising him to remove the sculpture in four days or see the City give it to charity or discard it. A very upset Goto was later allowed up to 30 days to find the sculpture a new home. Rhode Island College agreed to provide that home and placed the sculpture on campus in a grassy knoll at the rear of the college's art center. That site was recently developed by the college, and is now the site of the new Alex and Ani building. At this writing, the sculpture sits in storage as part of RIC's permanent collection awaiting assignment to its new location on campus which has yet to be determined.

Chapter 4

Johnson & Wales University

8 Abbott Park Place

MORRIS GAEBE

Morris Gaebe and his wife Audrey comprised one of the two visionary couples who transformed Johnson & Wales University into an institution with a national reputation for excellence. The University honored Morris with a bronze statue in 1998. (Photo by Paul Caranci)

EDWARD TRIANGOLO

Edward Triangolo and his wife Vilma complete the power couple behind the J &W transformation. They helped grow the 125 student school into an internationally recognized university with over 12,000 students from every state in the US and in excess of 70 countries. The University dedicated his statue in 2001. (Photo by Paul Caranci)

Like politics, time served in the United States Navy can make for proverbial strange bed fellows. That is where Illinois native Morris "Moe" Gaebe and Rhode Islander Edward Triangolo, two boys with little in common, became best friends. It was Triangolo's wife Vilma though that is probably most responsible for this unlikely pair becoming entrepreneurial legends of American higher education. Looking at the friends she said, "You two fellows don't have a post-war career. Why don't you buy the school?"[12] The "school" Vilma was referring to was a small business school started on September 14, 1914, by two women with a dream; Gertrude Irene Johnson and Mary Tiffany Wales. Their vision was to provide a program of business and office education "not for its own sake, but as preparation for what lies beyond."[13]

Edward and Vilma Triangolo did indeed partner with Morris and Audrey Gaebe to acquire the 125 student school in 1947, adding courses in business management, marketing, salesmanship and accounting. Together, the four entrepreneurs taught class, managed the office and cleaned the building. On a shoestring they worked indefatigably to grow the school and when enrollment dipped, Edward and Morris researched job data, scoured the classifieds and anticipated future job trends. They responded quickly to their research by restructuring programs and adding courses that would enable their graduates to land high-demand jobs.

The new owners wanted not only to prepare high school graduates for employment in the real world, but women and returning war veterans as well. Their idea was to teach the student who isn't going to one of the Ivy League schools and give them a chance for the degree that would lead to a life-long career.

Gaebe's and Triangolo's dedication to hard work, their entrepreneurial spirit and their understanding of what young people needed to succeed combined to create a period of unmatched growth in the field of education. When many schools were experiencing declining enrollment, Gaebe and Triangolo grew a small Rhode Island-based school of 125 students into an internationally recognized university

---

[12] interview with Mark Patinkin reported in the ProJo on January 19, 1997
[13] RI state Senate resolution 2014 S 3084 celebrating the 100th anniversary of the founding of Johnson & Wales University

with more than 12,000 students from every state in the union and in excess of 70 foreign countries. They established campuses in South Carolina, Virginia, North Miami, Denver and North Carolina. They developed the first bachelor's degree program in Culinary Arts in the United States and crafted the upside down curriculum designed to prepare a student for a career even if that student makes it through only two years of college. In this program the first two years are about work training while the last two years provide a more general education.

Even in his golden years Gaebe was expanding the school telling Mark Patinkin in a Providence Journal interview that he tried to retire in 1992 moving with his wife Audrey to Florida to be near two of their sons and five of their grandchildren. "Two years later, he opened a new branch campus in North Miami," wrote Patinkin. "That's what Gaebe did in his retirement. Then he went back to work in Providence as chancellor."[14]

However non-traditional, it is clear that the educational vision of Gaebe and Triangolo works. As Morris Gaebe noted to Patinkin during the 1977 interview, with just two months left in the academic year, 98% of graduating seniors have jobs waiting.

Johnson and Wales University decided to honor Moe Gaebe (1998) and Ed Triangolo (2001), by commissioning statues of the two men whose vision, hard work and dedication made possible the transformation of the school from a small business college to one of the nation's renowned universities. Skylight Studios, Inc of Woburn, Massachusetts was selected to design and create a greater-than-life-size bronze statue of each man. Moe Gaebe is depicted seated on a granite base. He is wearing a classic 3-piece suit, his left leg crossed over his right exposing his wing-tip shoes, his hands crossed and resting on his leg.

Edward Triangolo stands on a bronze slab resting on a granite base. He has a broad smile and wears a classic man's suit with a bow tie. Both buttons of his suit jacket are fastened and his right hand is inserted in his right pocket. His left knee has a slight bend and he is sporting tasseled loafers on his feet.

---

[14] Mark Patinkin 1/19/97 ProJo column discussing his interview with Morris Gaebe

The statues are located on opposite sides of the walkway at the main gate of the quadrangle on the Providence campus. The statues of the two friends face each other as if they were still in deep conversation about the University's history and ideals.

Chapter 5

Rhode Island School of Design

2 College Street

ORPHEUS ASCENDING

The intriguing statue of Orpheus Ascending brings Greek mythology to life, capturing the very moment when an anxious Orpheus looks back at Eurydice too soon, condemning her to eternity in Hades. (Photo by Heather Caranci)

In 1963 Mrs. Murray S. Danforth approached Gilbert Franklin, the Chairman of Rhode Island School of Design's Division of Fine Arts, with a proposition. Mrs. Danforth, a descendant of one of the school's founders and Chairwoman of the Board of Trustees proposed the construction of a fountain in Frazier Terrace, a small park area being planned on the RISD campus in honor of its President John R. Frazier. As it turns out, it was an offer that Chairman Franklin couldn't pass up. He drafted three conceptual plans and this depiction of the mythical Orpheus attempting to rescue his lover Eurydice from Hades was chosen by Danforth.

The bronze fountain consists of three large figures standing on a spreading pond frond rising out of a fountain basin and though the artist has not revealed the statue's true meaning Robert Freeman and

Vivienne Lasky, authors of *Hidden Treasure: Public Sculpture in Providence*, suggest that the statue represents love forever lost with the disobedient Orpheus looking back only to see the guide Hermes leading Eurydice back to Hades.

According to the Greek myth, the musician Orpheus had the ability to charm anyone with his music. Overcome with grief upon discovering that his wife Eurydice had died from a viper bite he descends to the depths of hell to soften the heart of Hades and Persephone with his music. So strong is the power of his music that it overcomes death itself and they agree to allow Eurydice to return to earth on the condition that Orpheus walk in front of her and not look back until they *both* had reached the upper world. As he re-enters the world of the living, an anxious Orpheus looks back at Eurydice forgetting that she too must have entered the upper world before he could look back. She immediately vanishes from his site forever cast back into Hades.

The bronze fountain, the gift of Mrs. Danforth and the work of Gilbert Franklin, is the prominent feature of Frazier Terrace, a small two-tiered park area located just off of Benefit Street on the RISD campus.

DAYBREAK

The five shapes that comprise Daybreak may represent the five divisions of the Rhode Island School of Design. The artist, however, chose not to reveal the meaning so as to leave any interpretation to the viewer's imagination. (Photo by Heather Caranci)

This 1968 bronze is also the gift of RISD Board Chairwoman, Mrs. Murray Danforth, and the work of faculty member Gilbert Franklin. Monumental in scale, it consists of five shapes, spherical and semi-spherical in nature, all fitted together at a central nexus.

As is the case with Orpheus Ascending, the artist did not reveal any meaning probably preferring instead that it remain "hidden" and left to the viewer's interpretation. Once again, Freeman and Lasky are left to surmise that the five components may represent the five divisions of the Rhode Island School of Design.

This sculpture is well positioned in the small green space at the junction of Benefit St., Waterman Avenue and Angell Street where the old courthouse once stood.

Section II

Public and Private Buildings

Chapter 6

Rhode Island State House

One Capitol Hill

INDEPENDENT MAN

The Independent Man may well be one of the most recognizable of all of Rhode Island's public sculpture, but his "birth" very nearly didn't happen as early conceptual plans called for a statue of Roger Williams to grace the pinnacle of the State House. (Photo courtesy of the Office of the Secretary of State)

It was an exciting time for Rhode Island's elected leaders. For years the general assembly had been meeting at various times in Newport, Bristol, Kingston, East Greenwich and on Benefit Street in Providence. Now, plans were well underway for a single, permanent State House at 82 Smith Street, on a hill overlooking the capital city, just a stone's throw from the very spot where Roger Williams founded this great state some 259 years earlier. It was January 8, 1895 and members of the Rhode Island Historical society, at the annual meeting of their organization, excitedly discussed the recently announced plans for the new construction. Members unanimously adopted a resolution which read, "Resolved that in the opinion of the Rhode Island Historical Society a statue of Roger Williams should surmount the dome of the State House about to be erected..." The Roger Williams Society concurred and the resolution, along with all its supporting testimony, was presented to a meeting of the Board of State House Commissioners four days later. Before this venue however, the proposal didn't enjoy the same degree of unanimity. Instead, the Commissioners voted on July 17, 1899 to commission George T. Brewster, a professor from the Rhode Island School of Design who hailed from Massachusetts, to design a statue for $3,000 to be cast by the Gorham Manufacturing Company for $2,000 and perched on the lantern surmounting the dome. Additionally, the Commissioners voted to leave the detail of the statue to the professional architects.

The initial design suggested by the architectural firm of McKim, Mead and White was for an 11 foot bronze of a modestly dressed woman called "Hope" believing that she would represent the State's 200 year old motto with dignity. After much debate, however, the idea was rejected.

By October of that year the Providence Journal reported that the statue of Roger Williams, Rhode Island's independent man, had also been dropped in favor of a figure that would depict the concepts of sovereignty and freedom. Charles McKim, the project's chief architect who had final authority for the decision, was quoted as saying that a statue of Roger Williams standing 235 feet above street level would be simply "a voluntary association of pantaloons, jacket and hat." Additionally, it didn't seem appropriate from his point of view to have a man dressed in colonial garb atop a Renaissance structure.

• • •

Consequently on December 18, 1899, Brewster's design of a brawny, muscular man clad only in a loin cloth was mounted atop the State House. The figure's right arm is outstretched and in the clutches of his right hand is a 14' spear. His left hand is resting on the top of an anchor, the State's symbol. The gilded bronze cast produced by the Gorham Company weighs in at over 500 pounds and stands 11' tall. It consists of five sections riveted together. The bronze came from a statue of Simon Bolivar that was donated to the Gorham Company by the City of New York after its mayor had determined that the statue was not aesthetically pleasing. The Bolivar statue, which had been a gift to New York City from the government of Venezuela, was melted down and recast.

To Rhode Islanders, the newly cast statue represented the fortitude of Rhode Island's founder and the outstanding characteristic of its citizens. Brewster called his creation The Independent Man because it epitomized the independent spirit of Roger Williams. The Board of State House Commissioners agreed that The Independent Man was the essence of all things Rhode Island.

Perhaps in empathy with the citizens he watches over, The Independent Man's reign atop the State House has not always been easy. In 1927 he suffered a serious lightning strike that caused a significant amount of damage. The repairs were made with the statue in place, but it took 42 copper-plated staples to hold him together. In 1951 additional repairs were required and on August 9, 1975, in preparation for the Nation's Bicentennial celebrations, The Independent Man left his perch for the first time in over 75 years to receive extensive repairs that included a new coat of gold leaf which was provided by the Paul King Foundry in Johnston. Before returning to his place of honor at the State House, high atop the world's fourth largest unsupported marble dome, The Independent Man visited the Warwick Shopping Mall where visitors were treated to a once-in-a-lifetime chance to see him up close. Today, a replica of the Independent man sculpted by local artist Douglas Corsini, remains a permanent part of the Mall's display.

GENERAL NATHANAEL GREENE

One of General George Washington's most trusted Revolutionary leaders was Rhode Island's own General Nathanael Greene. His house still stands as a museum in Coventry and his sword and uniform epaulettes are showcased in the State House. (Photo courtesy of the Rhode Island State Archives, Preston Collection, C#858)

Nathanael Greene was born on August 7, 1742 in the Potowomut section of Warwick, RI the son of a Quaker farmer and businessman. His family was among the earliest settlers to the area helping to establish the Colony of Rhode Island. As a young boy with limited opportunity Greene demonstrated an incredible enthusiasm for education and even convinced his parents to procure the services of a private tutor to teach him Latin and advanced math. He operated an iron foundry that his father purchased in Coventry and used every available opportunity to read books which he purchased with his earnings. He even helped establish the first public school in Coventry.

In the years subsequent to his father's death in 1770, Nathanael developed an interest in the government and in the military, not something readily embraced by those of the Quaker faith. He won election to the Rhode Island general assembly where he established himself as a man of extraordinary common sense, sound reason and convincing judgment.

Though marrying Catharine Littlefield in July 1774, the approaching American Revolution found Greene preoccupied with the task of organizing the Kentish Guard, a local militia near his home in Coventry. His participation in their activities, however, was limited due to a slight limp that rendered him unable to march. He instead used his time to study military tactics and strategy and following the Battles of Lexington and Concord he was appointed Major General in the Rhode Island Army of Observation. In that role he led 1,600 Rhode Island troops, called to service by the RI General Assembly, in the siege of Boston.

It did not take long for George Washington to take note of Greene's talents and on June 22, 1775, Greene was commissioned a brigadier general in the Continental Army. Upon meeting Washington for the first time on July 4th, the two became instant friends. Following the British evacuation of Boston in March of the year next, Washington gave Greene the command of the city prior to sending him to Long Island where on August 9th, he was given command of the Island's Continental forces. By September Greene was in command of the Colonial forces in New Jersey and shortly thereafter American troops suffered the loss of two New York fortifications, Fort Washington in Manhattan and Fort Lee across the Hudson River. Almost three thousand men were captured and blame fell to Greene.

• • •

Washington did not lose confidence in his young general however. Rather he promoted Greene to quartermaster general on March 2, 1778 while allowing him, at Greene's insistence, to retain his combat command, leading his troops in the Battle of Monmouth immediately upon departing Valley Forge where the army had wintered. In August of 1778, Washington sent Greene home to Rhode Island with the Marquis de Lafayette to strategize with Comte d'Estaing, a French Admiral, but the ensuing engagement ended in defeat on August 29 under the command of Brigadier General John Sullivan.

In June of 1780, Greene led his army in the more successful Battle of Springfield. Despite the victory, Greene became disgruntled with what he considered Congressional interference and just two months after Springfield, Greene resigned his commission as Quartermaster General. Meanwhile, American forces were reeling following a serious defeat in the Battle of Camden. Congress asked Washington to select a new commander for the southern region and he again turned to Greene, this time appointing him to lead Continental forces in the entire south. Greene took up his charge over a battered southern army on December 2, 1780.

Almost immediately he came upon the British forces under the direction of General Charles Cornwallis. Greene wisely chose to avoid the temptation of an immediate confrontation with Cornwallis providing him the chance to rebuild his army. Splitting his army in two, one of his leaders, Brigadier General Daniel Morgan engaged the enemy in the Battle of Cowpens and impressed with a brilliant victory. This conflict bought Greene enough time to reorganize his troops for the ultimate engagement with Cornwallis, one that took place on March 15th at the Battle of Guilford Court House. Greene's men were eventually forced to retreat, but not before inflicting heavy casualties on Cornwallis's troops forcing them to withdraw toward Wilmington, NC. Cornwallis, however, decided to move north toward Virginia allowing Greene's forces to move south and retake North and South Carolina for the Colonists at the same time trapping the Cornwallis troops in Charleston where they remained in containment until the end of the war.

In August of 1783, with victory in hand and Congress meeting in Princeton, Greene left the southern theater and surrendered his final commission. He returned to his home state of Rhode Island to a warm and hospitable reception but his stay was short-lived as North Carolina, South Carolina and Georgia all awarded him large grants of land in gratitude for his liberating service to their cause. By 1785, however, Greene had sold most of his land to repay his debts retiring to his plantation at Mulberry Grove along the banks of the Savannah River. There, with his wife and children, he looked forward to the contentment of a farming life. In fact, he was twice offered the post of Secretary of War and twice turned down the offer so he could farm with his family.

On June 12, 1786, while returning from a business trip, Greene stopped at a friend's plantation to discuss the possibility of producing rice at Mulberry Grove. He and his friend remained in the fields under a scorching sun for many hours before Greene departed for home. Once at home, he became very ill from the effects of sun stroke. The man who helped General Washington to victory in the Revolution died on June 19th at the age of 44, surrounded by a loving family. A shocked Savannah suspended all business activity upon learning the news and the entire nation mourned.

Many tributes were cast in Greene's honor and memory in various parts of the young country. There is a postage stamp in his honor and his "Homestead" along the banks of Rhode Island's Pawtuxet River remains a museum to this day. There are countless parks across America named in tribute to Greene and four Coast Guard revenue cutters were named for him as was a US Navy James Madison-class nuclear submarine (decommissioned in 1986). In addition, a Liberty class steam merchant (1942), and a 128' Army tug still in service today bear his name. There is a statue of Greene in the National Hall of Statuary in the nation's capital and a bronze equestrian statue at the center of Stanton Park in Washington, DC. There is a second equestrian statue in Greensboro, NC and a standing statue in a traffic circle between Greene and McGee Streets in that city. Tennessee named the town of Greeneville for him. South

Carolina honored him with the naming of Greenville and the unveiling of his statue at the corner of South Main and Broad Streets. In 2000, sculptor Chas Fagan unveiled a 6' bronze statue of Greene in St. Clair Park, Greensburg, PA.

Rhode Island honors Greene with a large oil painting in the State Room of the State House and a larger-than-life figure on one of two pedestals that flank the front entrance of the majestic edifice. The life-sized standing bronze statue was designed by Henri Schonhardt, a long-time employee of the Gorham Company which cast the statue in 1930. Dedicated in 1931, the cloaked statue of Greene faces front in a static position. His left hand rests on his sword hilt while he clutches gloves with his left.

As of this writing, The Nathanael Greene Monument Foundation is currently mounting a fundraising drive to provide the $300,000 necessary to erect a 22' tall statue of Greene, modeled after the equestrian in Greensboro, NC. They hope to unveil the latest tribute in 2016.

OLIVER HAZARD PERRY

Oliver Hazard Perry is honored for his heroics in the War of 1812's Battle of Lake Erie. There, despite being outmanned, Perry outmaneuvered British Commander Robert Barclay capturing his entire flotilla. (Photo by Heather Caranci)

The path to fame for Oliver Hazard Perry was frustrating and arduous, but perseverance and well placed connections provided an opportunity for Perry to showcase his talents and abilities causing history to forever remember him as the Hero of Lake Erie.

Oliver was born August 23, 1785 in the village of Wakefield, South Kingstown to Captain Christopher and Sarah (Alexander) Perry. One of eight children, Oliver was both strong-willed and quick tempered and enjoyed a love of the sea. At age 12 he sailed with his father to the West Indies and by 13 decided on a naval career. To realize his ambition, however, he would need a midshipman's warrant, something not easily attained. Yet on April 7, 1799, Perry was warranted a midshipman upon the recommendation of his father.

The initial six years of his career were uneventful. He served on famous ships and participated in the Quasi-War with France and the Tripolitan War against the Barbary Pirates, but was not involved in any memorable engagements. Following a two year leave, Perry was assigned the task of overseeing construction of a flotilla of small gunboats in Rhode Island and neighboring Connecticut. Though he loathed the task and thought it boring, it was an experience that would provide invaluable training for what was to come later.

In April, 1809, Perry received his first command as captain of the 14-gun schooner *Revenge* where he sailed the northern Atlantic as part of the Commodore John Rodgers' squadron. In the spring of 1810, in preparation for assignment in the southern Atlantic, Perry's ship was ordered to the Washington Navy Yard to repair damage it had previously suffered during a storm off the coast of Charleston, NC. The extreme hot and humid southern weather conditions, however, were not conducive to Perry's health and he was plagued with illness. By July, he was forced to request a transfer which was granted. Perry was ordered to conduct harbor surveys of New London, CT, Newport, RI and Gardiner's Bay, NY. However, on January 8, 1811, Perry's command of the *Revenge* came to an end. On that night, under heavy fog, he was forced to order the ship abandoned when it struck a reef near Watch Hill Point in Block Island Sound. A subsequent mandatory court martial exonerated Perry of any wrongdoing in the sinking.

After the incident, Perry took a much needed leave to marry Newport native Elizabeth Champlin Mason on May 5th and remained unemployed for a year following the couple's return from their honeymoon.

Before long, however, the potential for conflict with Britain drew him back to the Navy seeking a sea-going assignment, which he received upon the outbreak of the War of 1812. Though given command of a gunboat flotilla at Newport, RI, Perry was frustrated. He longed for the real action and the chance at glory and fame. Even a promotion to master commandant in October 1812 didn't satisfy his lust for action and he continued to badger the Navy Department for a sea-going assignment. He contacted his friend, Commodore Isaac Chauncey, who, as luck would have it, was desperate for someone with Perry's experience to assist him in his command of US naval forces on the Great Lakes. Though not overly excited by an assignment that didn't include the Atlantic, Perry accepted the transfer in February 1813 and took command of the small fleet being built on Lake Erie.

Perry's frustration only grew, however, when he realized that ship construction plans were far less complete than he had been led to believe. He worked indefatigably in a race with his British counterpart Commander Robert Barclay to ready the ships ultimately completing work on a fleet that included the brigs *USS Lawrence* and *USS Niagara* as well as seven smaller vessels. With Perry at the helm of the *Lawrence*, the flotilla deployed to Lake Erie before the British were ready. The flag that was proudly flown atop the *Lawrence* displayed the words of ship namesake and Perry friend, Captain James Lawrence; "Don't Give Up the Ship."

On September 10th, Perry and Barclay finally met on the massive lake in what was to become known as the Battle of Lake Erie. Though initially being overwhelmed by Barclay's forces, and with the *Lawrence* in a battered state, Perry boarded a small boat and transferred to the *Niagara* that had just joined the engagement. Perry skillfully used the *Niagara* to alter the trend of the battle and secured the capture of Barclay's entire flotilla. Perry reported the success to General William Henry Harrison, already famous for his own impressive victory at Tippicanoe, with the now immortal words, "We have met the enemy and they are ours."

Perry did not rest on his victory at Erie, however. He quickly used his fleet to ferry Harrison's army of the Northwest to Detroit where it began its advance into Canada, a campaign that culminated with the October 5, 1813 victory in the Battle of the Thames. With victory of the Lakes secured, and hero status thrust upon him, Perry was promoted to Captain and finally sailed for home in Rhode Island.

In July of the following year, he was given command of the USS Java, a new frigate which was being constructed in Baltimore, MD. He presided over the construction project and remained in the city during the British attacks on North Point and Fort McHenry in September. He feared the loss of his still unfinished ship during the attacks, but secured her safety. Unfortunately for the man who longed for action, his ship wasn't ready until after the war ended.

Perry participated in the Second Barbary War in 1815 but while in the Mediterranean, Perry and Java's Marine officer, John Heath, had an argument that escalated until Perry slapped Heath. Both were court-martialed and reprimanded, and the two carried a grudge well into 1817 when, on October 19th Heath challenged Perry to a duel. The encounter took place on the same field where Aaron Burr ended the life of Alexander Hamilton in a similar show of manhood. Heath fired first from a distance of only 4 paces and missed. Perry, well within his right to kill Heath, refused to pull the trigger proving him truly worthy of his hero status.

During the same period, Perry and another nemesis from Lake Erie, Jesse Duncan Elliott, exchanged harsh words via letters prompting Elliott to challenge Perry to a duel. Rather than accept, Perry filed a formal court-martial charge against him for "Conduct unbecoming an officer, manifesting disregard for the honor of the American flag, and failure to 'do his utmost to take or destroy the vessel of the enemy which it was his duty to encounter.'"

Not wanting to sully the good name of either officer, each of whom was well connected, the Secretary of the Navy turned the question over to President James Monroe who simply diffused the situation by suppressing the whole matter and choosing Perry to command a diplomatic mission to South America.

Perry initially sailed aboard the *U.S. John Adams* but transferred to the *USS Nonsuch* at the mouth of the Orinoco River, arriving in Angostura, the Venezuelan capitol on July 27th. Yellow fever was rampant in that area and despite twenty of his crewman contracting the disease, four of whom died, Perry completed his mission and departed Venezuela on August 15th in good health. Two days later, however, Perry was awakened at 4:00 in the morning with chills and a high fever. His condition worsened quickly and at 3:00 in the afternoon of Monday, August 23, 1819, only a few miles from medical help at the Port of Spain, Perry died aboard the vessel from yellow fever. It was his 34th birthday.

Like Nathanael Greene, Perry was honored in many ways in many parts of the nation. No less than eight ships were christened in his honor, the most recent being the SSV Oliver Hazard Perry, an educational tall ship, launched in 2013. Statues of Perry are prominent in Erie, Pennsylvania (1925) and in Eisenhower Park in Newport, RI (1885). Additional monuments to his honor were erected at Put-In-Bay, OH, Erie, PA, Buffalo, NY and Cleveland, OH. A $1 postage stamp was issued in his honor in 1894 and a Victory and International Peace Memorial Quarter in 2013.

At the Rhode Island State House, on a pedestal originally intended for a light post, stands a majestic life-sized bronze of Perry dressed in his navy uniform, clutching a sword in his right hand, with an anchor at his right side. The statue was designed by William Walcutt, cast by the Gorham Company, and dedicated in 1928. It is a replica of a marble statue sculpted by the same artist and dedicated in Cleveland, Ohio in 1860.

THE GARDEN OF HEROES

Dedicated in 2005, the Garden of Heroes was actually constructed during the 1997 filming of the Steven Spielberg production "Amistad" starring Morgan Freeman and Anthony Hopkins. For the film it was designed to replicate an 1840s congressional garden. Legislation converted it to a permanent memorial commemorating those who "gave the last full measure of devotion" in the various wars against terror since September 2001. (Photo by Paul Caranci)

Located on the southwest lawn of the State House, the Garden of Heroes honors the Rhode Island service members that gave their lives in support of the Global War on Terrorism since September 11, 2001. The principal feature is a large granite memorial with the names of the State's fallen carved in stone. Fourteen of the 27 names were original to the stone. The additional names were added at various intervals since the memorial's dedication on October 23, 2005. The Garden is centered around a large, silver, star-shaped planter, surrounded by smaller identity stones that commemorate each of the five branches of the United States military. There are two teak benches on either side of the Garden which is decorated with red, white and blue plantings. The memorial, originally constructed for filming of the motion picture "Amistad" and repurposed as a memorial to the State's fallen heroes through 2004 legislation, was designed and constructed with donated services, materials, labor and equipment and is maintained by volunteers with the assistance of the State House Facilities Department.

WWII SERVICEMEN COMMEMORATIVE STATUES
THE INFANTRYMAN

Italian Sculptor Guido Costanza was commissioned by Governor J. Howard McGrath in 1945 to design and sculpt six marble statues to adorn the walls of the 2nd floor of the State House. Collectively, the statues commemorate various branches of the US armed forces that served in World War II. (Photos by Paul Caranci)

• • •

THE SAILOR

THE AMERICAN PARATROOPER

THE ARMY ENGINEER

THE ARTILLERYMAN

THE ARMY AIRMAN

In 1945, Rhode Island Governor J. Howard McGrath, as part of a larger project that included redecoration of the inside of the Capitol dome, commissioned the sculpting of six statues to be placed in the "niches" decorating the walls of the second floor of the State House. Providence Artist and interior decorator George DeFelice was given a contract to supervise the various phases of the project while noted sculptor Guido Costanza of Rome, Italy, was assigned the task of sculpting six heroic figures representing various branches of the US armed forces serving in WWII.

Each of the six statues stand seven feet tall and are carved from pure white marble from the noted quarries of Carrara, in the province of Tuscany, Italy. They stand on pedestals each measuring three feet in height and made of pink polished marble. They were designed to match the background painting of the niches providing a striking contrast with the white marble figures.

Prior to sculpting the figures, Costanza, who established a studio at Carrara just for this work, checked with the US Consulate for accuracy of the uniforms and other statue details.

One of the statues depicts an *American paratrooper* with a parachute strapped to his back and a sub-machine gun, rifle and heavy belt of ammunition secured to his waist. A second statue is of an *Army engineer* carrying the surveying equipment he would have used in the performance of his duties. The statue of an *Army airman* is clothed in a Mae West jacket and has a parachute strapped to his back. In his hands is the steering gear from a war plane. The *infantryman* stands looking to his right and is dressed in a long coat with his hands clasped over the muzzle of a carbine placed in front of him. The Navy is represented by a *sailor* clutching a thick rope while standing bear foot with his pants rolled to mid-calf length as if stepping in low water. The sixth and final statue depicts an *Artilleryman* on patrol and looking upward raising a pair of binoculars toward his face.

The almost four-year long project was not complete until after McGrath left office to serve in the cabinet of President Harry S. Truman as Solicitor General of the United States. Lt. Governor John O. Pastore stepped up upon McGrath's resignation to complete the Governor's unfinished third term. It was Governor Pastore that presided over the February 9, 1949 dedication of the statues.

• • •

The plaques that bear the honor rolls of Rhode Island war dead, another component of the WWII Commemorative project, were added to the flanks of the State House Library at a later date.

THOMAS WILSON DORR

Thomas Wilson Dorr might be best remembered for his attempts to execute a new state constitution and the subsequent 1842 rebellion, but the People's Governor also secured the implementation of banking reforms and educational innovations. (Photo courtesy of Richard McCaffrey)

Dr. and Gail Conley pose with the statue of Thomas Wilson Dorr which they commissioned. Dr. Conley organized and presided over the November 5, 2014 dedication ceremony at the State House, the statue's permanent home. (Photo by Heather Caranci)

Deputy Secretary of State Paul F. Caranci, this book's co-author, delivered remarks at the State House dedication of the Thomas Wilson Dorr statue on November 5, 2014. (Photo courtesy of Richard McCaffrey)

Dr. & Mrs. Conley (left) and Paul & Heather Caranci (right) celebrated the November 5, 2014 dedication of the remarkable Joseph Avarista creation of Thomas Wilson Dorr in statue. (Photo courtesy of Richard McCaffrey)

The dedication ceremony unveiling the Thomas Wilson Dorr statue and its new pedestal and plaque was billed as a party celebrating the 209th year of Dorr's November 5, 1805 birth as well as his vindication day of November 5, 2014. (Photo courtesy of Richard McCaffrey)

Thomas Wilson Dorr grew up on Benefit Street on the City's East Side. Born to Sullivan and Lydia Allen Dorr on November 5, 1805, he spent his early years in a mansion built on land once owned by Roger Williams. In fact it was Williams' initial burial place in April 1683, but the internment was without ceremony and the grave was unmarked.

Sometime in 1860, it was decided that Williams' body should be exhumed so that he could be afforded the proper burial he so deserved. But when earth was removed beneath an apple tree in the corner of the yard where Williams was believed to be buried, all that was found was "greasy dirt" (a hint that a body had been there) and a root from the old apple tree. Oddly enough, the root eerily took on the shape of a man. "It curved where Roger's head should have been and entered the chest cavity, growing down the spine. It branched at the two legs, and then upturned into feet!"[15]

According to the legend, the apple tree absorbed Roger Williams' body into the root and the fruit of that tree, eaten by young Thomas Dorr, may have contributed to the rebellious nature for which he would become famous. Those employed at the RI Historical Society don't really believe that Roger Williams was absorbed by an apple tree, but they have taken custody of the root and now display it in the carriage house of the John Brown House at 52 Power Street, just a short distance from the Sullivan Dorr House.

As a boy, Thomas Dorr attended Phillips Exeter Academy and he graduated from Harvard in 1823. He studied law in New York under Chancellor James Kent and Vice-Chancellor William McCoun and was admitted to the bar in 1887 practicing in his home town of Providence. In 1834 he took a seat in the Rhode Island House of Representatives. During his tenure in the RI House, Dorr established himself as a reformer whose ideas were strenuously opposed by the Yankee establishment. He advocated loudly for several reforms that included the adoption of a new constitution to replace the 180 year old Colonial Charter procured by Dr. John Clarke in 1663, better apportionment of the state legislature and for universal male suffrage.

---

[15]Tree Root That Ate Roger Williams—**www.roadsideamerica.com/story/2210 1996-2014** Doug Kirby, Ken Smith, Mike Wilkins

He also secured the implementation of banking reforms and educational innovations. His reform efforts were consistently blocked by the state legislature and by 1841 Rhode Island was one of the only states that had not adopted a new constitution that included universal suffrage for white males including Irish Catholic naturalized citizens. The refusal to accept his ideas meant that less than ½ of the male population in Rhode Island was eligible to vote and legislators from only 19 towns with a total population of 3,500 comprised over ½ of the legislature. In fact, less than 1,800 voters essentially made all the decisions for the state's 108,000 people.

Frustrated, in 1841 Dorr joined the Rhode Island Suffrage Association which called for a constitutional convention, adopted a constitution that included many of Dorr's reforms and submitted it to the people for a vote. Nearly fourteen thousand ballots were cast in favor of the constitution while only 32 people voted against it. While Dorr's election was open to non-landowning males not otherwise eligible to vote, over 4,900 of the votes were cast by those considered to be qualified voters under the Colonial Charter. The so-called Law and Order Party, led by Governor Samuel Ward King and other "traditional constitutionalists" refused to recognize the new party or its constitution which the Dorrites had already put into effect. They held elections in May of 1842 in which Dorr was elected Governor. Other state officers and a new legislature were elected as well. Governor King, who was re-elected in a competing set of elections held a few weeks later, appealed to the RI Supreme Court which ruled in his favor calling the actions of Thomas Dorr and his People's Party treasonous.

Arrest warrants were issued for Dorr and his followers who were locked out of the State House. Undeterred, Dorr mobilized his forces, stole cannon from the Benefit Street Armory that were left over from the Revolutionary War, and led a charge on the state arsenal. On May 18, 1842, with Dorr's uncle and younger brother inside the Arsenal defending Governor King's position, Dorr attempted to fire the cannon. Perhaps the night's dampness prevented the cannon from firing. Perhaps it was the age of the cannon or maybe it was God's providence that was responsible for the lack of bloodshed that night. Whichever the cause, the misfire was enough to send many of Dorr's men scurrying in all directions. The rebellion was over almost before it had begun, but in the aftermath, Dorr would flee the state, return to convene the People's legislature in Chepachet only to disband his forces and turn himself in to the authorities.

Dorr was tried for treason, convicted and sentenced to life of hard labor in prison. He was committed to the state prison in Providence on June 27, 1844. It may well have been his family's status the prevented Justice Job Durfee's court from imposing the death penalty on Dorr. That same influence may have helped soften the legislature to the public opinion that demanded Dorr's release, for in 1845, an Act of General Amnesty was passed and Dorr was released just 12 months into his prison term. In 1851 his civil rights were restored and in 1854 the verdict of the Supreme Court was annulled though the court ruled that action unconstitutional.

Though suffering from his self-imposed temporary exile and eventual loss of liberty, Dorr did get to enjoy at least a symbolic victory in when in 1843 the state adopted a new constitution that included some of the reforms that he sacrificed so much for. Today, Dorr is accepted more as a reformer than a rebel and his portrait, painted by Wilfred I. Duphiney, proudly hangs on the walls of the State House among those of the other governors elected to lead Rhode Island. Unlike any of Rhode Island's other governors however, Dorr has a life-size, full length statue standing guard outside the State House's Senate Chamber thanks to the efforts of RI Historian Laureate Dr. Patrick Conley and his wife Gail.

Dr. Conley, a long-time supporter of Dorr and his reform efforts, commissioned Jamestown, RI sculptor Joseph A. Avarista to carve a statue of Dorr out of a half-ton block of basswood for placement at the entrance of the proposed Heritage Harbor Museum. Though the museum was never built, that statue was completed in 2004. The life-like, oil painted recreation stands 6'4" tall including its base and is clad in traditional mid-19th century suit and frock. The frock hangs open in front exposing the fastened buttons of the suit jacket beneath. His right hand clutches a rolled scroll symbolizing the People's Constitution and hangs by his side while his left hand holds Chancellor Kent's Commentaries on American Law with the arm bent at the elbow at almost 90 degrees. The top portion of the pedestal is painted to resemble a Persian rug. The statue found a home at Dr. Conley's Fabre Line Club from 2008 until 2014 when he donated it for display at the Rhode Island State House.

● ● ●

On Tuesday, January 7, 2014, Dr. Conley, his wife Gail and Avarista joined Governor Lincoln Chafee, Secretary of State A. Ralph Mollis, Senate President M. Teresa Paiva Weed, House Speaker Gordon Fox and many other dignitaries and attendees at an unveiling ceremony in front of the Senate Chamber. The statue now stands in the very spot left vacant by the removal of the 1663 Colonial Charter to its new home in the newly created Charter Museum one floor below. As Dr. Conley noted, Thomas Dorr, for the second time, replaces the Colonial Charter!

The statue of Dorr was officially dedicated at an impressive ceremony on November 5, 2014, the 209th anniversary of Dorr's birth. The State House ceremony included the presentation of the plaque and pedestal on which the likeness stands. Speakers included Jonathan Stevens, Executive Director of the RI 1663 Colonial Charter Commission who gave the greetings of Governor Lincoln Chafee, and Paul F. Caranci, Rhode Island Deputy Secretary of State. The keynote address was given by Dr. Patrick T. Conley, Rhode Island's Historian Laureate. The base and plaque were paid with private funds provided by Dorr's present-day admirers and raised by Dr. and Mrs. Patrick Conley.

ELIZABETH BUFFUM CHASE

One of the most prominent figures in the 19th century effort to provide slaves a passage to the freedom of Canada was Elizabeth Buffum Chase. Selected for honor by Secretary of State Edward S. Inman and his Deputy Ray Rickman, she is commemorated in this 2001 bust sculpted by Pablo Edwardo and is the first woman to be so honored in statue at the State House. Following the Civil War and passage of the Emancipation Proclamation, Chase became a strong advocate for political rights for women as well as prison and workplace reform. (Photo by Paul Caranci)

● ● ●

Elizabeth Buffum was born in Smithfield, RI on December 9, 1806. Her parents, Arnold Buffum and Rebecca Gould, both strong anti-slavery Quakers, were among the oldest families in New England. On April 4, 1828, Elizabeth married Samuel Buffington Chase of similar birthright.

Together, the couple opened their home at the corner of Hunt and Broad Streets (no longer standing) in Central Falls, RI to runaway slaves as a Station of the Underground Railroad. From there, the couple helped the slaves escape to Canada. While exposing themselves to the tremendous dangers that came along with such a noble cause, the couple also suffered great personal tragedy as the first five of their ten children died as a result of childhood diseases that ravaged families of the time.

The Chaces continued their efforts to eradicate slavery and when the Civil War broke out in 1861, though firmly supportive of the Union cause, expressed their disappointment that President Lincoln did not emancipate the slaves at the outset. Throughout the time, Elizabeth corresponded routinely with some of the most significant anti-slavery figures of the day, including Frederick Douglass, William Wells Brown and William Lloyd Garrison, all of whom were regular guests at her home.

Elizabeth remained a strong advocate for noble causes long after the Civil War had ended advocating for political rights of woman as well as prison and workplace reform. She died on December 12, 1899 and is remembered today as one of the 19th century's most influential anti-slavery, woman's rights and prison reform activists.

In 2001, RI Secretary of State Edward S. Inman selected Elizabeth Buffum Chace from a field of 36 nominees to be the first woman honored in the Rhode Island State House. He did so with the placement of a bronze bust. Chosen for this honor even before Anne Hutchinson and Christiana Carteaux Bannister, Buffum Chase is depicted in bronze as "The Conscience of Rhode Island" for her tireless championing of the rights of the less fortunate. The very act of creating a bust of Chase is symbolic because only major figures of society, particularly Roman emperors and patriarchs, were depicted in such a way in ancient times. The bust is the 2002 creation of sculptor Pablo Eduardo and can be found in a small alcove on the 2nd floor of the State House.

• • •

THEODORE FRANCIS GREEN

The very powerful former RI Governor Theodore Francis Green retired from the United States Senate in 1962 at the age of 94. He was at the time the oldest serving member of the Senate. This mastermind of Rhode Island's Bloodless Revolution facilitated the alteration of the face of Ocean State politics for generations. (Photo by Paul Caranci)

It was an emotional scene when 94 year old Theodore Francis Green, the oldest member of the United States Senate, rose to explain to his colleagues the reason for his resignation.

He had risen to amazing heights, serving as Chairman of the Senate's Foreign Relations Committee, one of the most powerful Washington, DC posts, but time had finally caught up with the man once described as "the most enthusiastic party-goer in the Capitol" and one who would walk four miles every day. He told his colleagues that on this day he did not walk to his office but rather shared a cab ride in, though he hadn't lost all common sense as "he let the other riders pay."[16]

Green was born in Providence on October 2, 1867 to parents descendent from colonists who arrived in Rhode Island with Roger Williams. He was educated in Providence schools, graduated from Brown in 1887 and attended Harvard Law School, the University of Bonn and the University of Berlin.

Never married, Green's life was devoted to law and politics. He was admitted to the Bar in 1892 and served as a first Lieutenant in command of a provisional infantry company during the Spanish-American War. His political career began with election to the RI House of Representatives in 1907. He eagerly began his efforts to re-form state politics and government through ethnic unification and modernization. He served as Chairman of his Democrat Party's State Committee and as a delegate to Democratic National Conventions. After three unsuccessful campaigns for Governor and one for the US House of Representatives, he finally won election as Rhode Island's governor in 1932 serving two terms.

In 1935 he masterminded "the bloodless revolution" success-fully wresting control from the Republican Party which unabashedly held power for decades. The events led to the rise of the modern, dom-inant Democrat Party in Rhode Island.

Among his accomplishments, Governor Green focused on welfare and unemployment relief during the Great Depression and his relief bill was signed three weeks ahead of President Roosevelt's New

---

[16]Quahog.org Facts and folklore – Theodore Francis Green by Florence Markoff – The story of his resignation from the United States Senate.

Deal. He also increased the power of the Governor's office through an intensive reorganization. The result of his efforts was a landslide victory to the United States Senate in 1936. In Washington, Green was intensely partisan supporting domestic New Deal measures and some controversial measures, such as the Supreme Court Retirement bill, for which he incurred the wrath of his constituents.

He supported laws providing for absentee voting of WWII servicemen and opposed attempts to exempt farm workers from the draft. He also secured passage of a law releasing government-owned silver for war purposes. He faithfully and constantly advocated for civil rights legislation, enacting laws to ban the poll tax and to make lynching a federal crime. He also helped President Lyndon Johnson secure eastern liberal support for the Civil Rights Act of 1957.

Green died in Providence on May 19, 1966, just four years after retiring from his beloved US Senate. In his honor, a bronze bust was commissioned for placement in the State House. It was sculpted by Margaret Chambers Gould who did a second bust for display at the Warwick, RI airport that bears his name. The armless bust shows Green, hair parted in the middle, wearing a vest, tie and suit jacket. The bronze is displayed on the second floor of the State House opposite the entrance to the House of Representatives where Green once served.

J. HOWARD MCGRATH

After reorganizing Rhode Island's juvenile court system, sponsoring a workers' compensation fund and a labor relations board, Governor J. Howard McGrath resigned his office in 1945 to accept a presidential appointment as Solicitor General of the United States. He was later appointed to the cabinet of President Harry S. Truman serving as US Attorney General. (Photo by Paul Caranci)

James Howard McGrath was born to James J and Ida E. (May) McGrath in Woonsocket on November 28, 1903. He graduated from LaSalle Academy, Providence College (1922) and Boston University Law School (1929). A few months after his graduation, on November 28th he married Estelle A. Cadorette.

He began his political apprenticeship in 1930 with a four year stint as the Central Falls City Solicitor and served as United States Attorney from 1934 to 1940. Following that he began a campaign for Governor.

McGrath took office as Rhode Island's 60th Governor on January 7, 1941. During his tenure he reorganized the juvenile court system and sponsored a workers' compensation fund and a labor relations board. Though winning reelection in both 1942 and 1944, McGrath would serve as Governor for less than five years. On October 6, 1945, mid way through his third term, McGrath resigned his position to accept appointment as Solicitor General of the United States. In 1946 McGrath won a position in the United States Senate, a year in which the opposition Republican Party took control of both houses. While in the Senate he opposed reducing wartime economic controls. He also opted to increase spending for Social Security, national health insurance and education in lieu of a tax decrease.

From 1947 to 1949 McGrath chaired the Democratic National Committee where he managed President Truman's successful 1948 election campaign. On August 24, 1949, McGrath accepted a presidential appointment as United States Attorney General, a coveted cabinet level position but was asked by Truman to resign on April 3, 1952 when he refused to cooperate in a corruption investigation begun by his own department. McGrath was one of only two Rhode Islander's appointed to cabinet level positions. The other was John Chafee who was appointed Secretary of the Navy by President Richard Nixon.

McGrath retreated to private law practice in Washington, D.C. and Providence but tried to revive his political career with an unsuccessful run for the US Senate when Theodore Francis Green announced his retirement in 1960.

On September 2, 1966, McGrath suffered a fatal heart attack in Narragansett, RI. In 1977 a bronze bust was made in his honor and placed in the State House. It is located on the 2nd floor just outside the entrance to the House of Representatives.

• • •

CHRISTIANA CARTEAUX BANNISTER

Only the second woman honored in statue at Rhode Island's State House, Christiana Carteaux Bannister risked her life to use her hair salon as a meeting place for African Americans and white abolitionists participating in the Underground Railroad. She also advocated for equal pay for Black soldiers fighting in the Civil War and founded a Home for Aged Colored Women who were homeless following their work as domestics. (Photo by Paul Caranci)

Born Christiana Babcock circa 1819, this North Kingstown native was descendant of enslaved Africans. Her parents most likely were of African American and Narragansett Indian descent. Christiana move to Boston while still a young woman where she worked as a wigmaker and hairdresser and married a clothes dealer named Desiline Carteaux, believed to be of Caribbean origin.

Christiana emerged as a successful business person opening several salons under the name of Madame Carteaux. Her marriage, however, was short-lived and in 1857 she remarried to Edward Mitchell Bannister, a barber who worked in her Boston salon. He went on to become a wildly successful artist, in fact, one of the most successful Black artists, in large part due to Christiana's financial and emotional support.

In 1869, the couple moved to Providence. Christiana opened another salon and supplemented her work as a hairdresser with political activism, something she began in Boston when she used her hair salon as a meeting place for African Americans and white abolitionists participating in the Underground Railroad. Now, her activism extended to equal pay for Black soldiers during the Civil War. She also founded the Home for Aged Colored Women who were homeless because they were now too old to continue their work as domestics. Located on Dodge Street, the home was renamed Bannister House, Inc.

Christiana died in 1902, ironically while a resident in the Bannister Center that she established. She is buried in a plot with her husband in the North Burial Ground. In December of 2002 a statue was dedicated to her at the RI State House. The bronze bust was sculpted by Pablo Eduardo and is based upon a portrait that was done of Christiana by her husband.

Chapter 7

The Dorrance Restaurant Building

60 Dorrance Street

THE PILGRIM & THE PURITAN

One of the least common forms of sculpture, according to RI historian William McKenzie Woodward, is what he terms idealized sculpture – those representing idealistic memorials to an idea or historic figure. The Puritan and the Pilgrim above the doorway of the building located at 60 Dorrance Street is a beautiful example of this rare form. (Photo by Paul Caranci)

Rhode Island historian William McKenzie Woodward, in his introduction to *Hidden Treasure: Public Sculpture in Providence* notes the various categories of the city's public monuments; those that commemorate a person or major event, idealistic memorials to an idea or historic figure and decorative pieces for parks or gardens.

Of these categories, idealized sculpture may be the least common in Providence, but, as Woodward points out, "they are well known to most Americans." There are several illustrations of idealized sculpture in Providence as portrayed in this and the following four chapters.

The carved figures of the Puritan and the Pilgrim that lie in the arched doorway on either side of the center cornice of the former Union Trust Building idealize the relationship established between the new colonists and their Native American hosts, two cultures that defined New England's history. Yet just as poignant in this depiction is the fact that the two figures face opposite directions, perhaps indicative of the underlying hostilities that would eventually arise between the two very different and distinct cultures represented by each. The carvings are the work of Daniel Chester French and were completed in 1902. Over the course of the years subsequent to its completion in 1901, this building served as a financial institution and a restaurant. Prior to the opening of Dorrance Restaurant, the facility was host to the Federal Reserve Restaurant.

Chapter 8

Providence City Hall

25 Dorrance Street

ROGER WILLIAMS

Looking down from its perch in the arched frieze above the massive front doors of City Hall is a granite carving of the State's founder, Roger Williams. There were no paintings done of Roger Williams during his lifetime and no one really knows what he may have looked like. (Photo by Heather Caranci)

That Providence was in need of a new building from which to administer its local government was obvious. Where that new city hall should be located, however, was not. The long simmering political controversy did not end with the purchase of the so called city hall lot at the corner of Dorrance and Washington Streets. In fact, that purchase did nothing to settle the issue as the council decided to lease the newly acquired parcel rather than build on it. Eventually, C.N. Harrington (the lessor) built a two-story wood frame structure on the land that was used as a theater, hosting concerts and plays over the next 20 years.

In 1874, a overwhelming majority of the city council, one that had different members than the council that leased the land 20 years earlier, broke ranks with Mayor Thomas Doyle overriding his veto of the use of these lots for a municipal government building. Ground was finally broken for the new City Hall on April 24, 1875.

A design competition drew 21 entries from which a plan submitted by Boston native Samuel J. F. Thayer was selected. Cost overruns inflated the $635,000 budget to $1.1 million but the final result was a beautiful five-story, fireproof structure that stood in design among the most advanced in the world. The foundation was built on 3,128 piles driven to bedrock because the structure was built on land that was once part of the Cove Tidal Water basin. Constructed with iron and brick, the building is faced with Westerly granite on the east and north sides and New Hampshire granite on the other two sides. The 133' by 160' building was dedicated on November 14, 1878.

Included in the list of dignitaries who have addressed large crowds from the front steps of this city hall building are President Theodore Roosevelt, who delivered the "Trust" speech on August 23, 1902, and presidential candidate John F. Kennedy who addressed a crowd from the same location on November 7, 1960, his last campaign speech before his historic election.

Perhaps a most fitting inclusion in the structure is the granite carving of the State's founder, Roger Williams. From his perch in the arched frieze over the massive front doors protected within a circled medallion, Williams is depicted in bust dressed in traditional colonial garb with a large hat atop his head.

Chapter 9

Federal Courthouse

2 Exchange Terrace

AMERICA

The two statue groups that flank the entrance of the federal building opposite City Hall are called Providence (to the left of the doorway) and America (to the right). The sculptures were designed by John Massey Rhind who once cast bronze for the Gorham Company. These are thought to be the best example of turn of the century carved sculpture developed with Beaux-Arts architecture and used in public buildings. (Photos by Heather Caranci)

• • •

PROVIDENCE

Flanking the doorway of the Federal Post Office Building located opposite Providence City Hall in Kennedy Plaza and named in honor of former RI Governor and US Senator John O. Pastore, are two massive statue groups measuring thirteen feet in height. Carved in white marble, this work of John Massey Rhind depicts the allegorical female figures arranged in pyramidal compositions. The statues were carved in 1908 and were quite likely inspired by The Four Continents on the New York Customs House designed by Daniel Chester French in 1906 and immediately recognized as masterpieces.

The Federal Building itself was designed as a result of a competition promoted by the United States Treasury Department in 1903. It is a Beaux-Arts neoclassical four-story structure with colossal Corinthian colonnades, modillion cornice, and balustrade parapet. It is a magnificent example in which the statues are designed as an essential part of the structure's façade. This distinction sets it apart from most of the other sculptures in the City.

The building site is also quite significant as it was here that Abraham Lincoln spoke to a crowd of people on the evening of February 28, 1860 after delivering his famous Cooper Union speech in New York. This was one of only two official Lincoln visits to Rhode Island and a plaque on the buildings southwest corner commemorates that event.

To the left of the center doorway is Providence, symbolized by Independent Thought. The allegorical figure holds a branch of maple leaves in her right hand and an open book in her left. Kneeling at her left side is Knowledge, a female figure that is reading a large book opened almost to the center page. The woman is wearing a shroud and is accompanied by an owl symbolizing Wisdom. Industry, a male figure wearing work shoes and pants is kneeling to the right of the central figure and holds a hammer in his right hand. His left hand rests on a pulley block.

The Massive statue to the right of the doorway is America, depicted by a seated female figure representing Sovereignty. On her head is a wreath of olive branches. Her left hand holds a bough of laurel and her right a globe topped with an eagle. The two figures on either side represent Justice (to Sovereignty's right) and Law & Order (to her left).

● ● ●

Justice, a female figure, has a balance on her lap and holds a sword of justice in her left hand. Law & Order is a male figure and is shown marking the page of a book with his left index finger.

John Massey Rhind was born in Scotland but trained in London and Paris. Prior to sculpting Providence and America, he cast bronze for the Gorham Company. With this massive work, thought to be Rhode Island's best example of turn of the century carved sculpture developed with Beaux-Arts architecture and used for public buildings, Rhind demonstrated his ability to visualize and effect figure groups in stone as well.

Chapter 10

Wayland Building

126 North Main Street

FRANCIS WAYLAND

This beautiful bronze bust of former Brown University President Francis Wayland rests in arched niche above the main door of the building located at 126 North Main Street that bears his name. (Photo by Paul Caranci)

Francis Wayland wasn't born in Rhode Island, but his contributions here were many and varied. Born in New York City on March 11, 1796, Wayland received his license to study medicine in early 1802 and was recognized for both his medical skills and his moral character. In 1816 he entered the Andover Theological Seminary, served as pastor of Boston's First Baptist Church for five years and founded the Newton Theological Institution in 1825.

Two years later Wayland began what would be a twenty-eight year reign as president of Brown University. During that time he presided over a period of structural and academic growth that included the formation of a library. He wrote books on a variety of subjects and became an advocate for temperance and anti-slavery causes as well as prison reform issues. He was a leader of the Law and Order Party during the years of the Dorr Rebellion and was often referred to as Rhode Island's "first citizen."

Wayland died in Providence on September 30, 1865 and is interred at the North Burial Ground. Just eight years later Charles P. Hartshorn constructed a building at 126 North Main Street in the City naming it in Wayland's honor. Long the home of Fain's Carpeting, Inc., the building includes an arched niche above the main door in which a marble bust of Wayland dressed in a classical manner is seen. The bust is mounted on a concrete base and is the work of Franklin Bachelder Simmons, a prominent nineteenth century American Sculptor.

Chapter 11

Turk's Head Building

76 Westminster Street

THE TURK'S HEAD

According to legend, this granite carving of "The Turk's Head" above the door of the building that bears its name commemorates the lost original placed by a man that owned a business at this very site. The original version of the Ottoman Warrior was retrieved from the ship Sultan and used by the owner to draw attention to his business in the days when few people could read a sign. (Photo by Paul Caranci)

In the heart of the downtown Providence financial district, in a small plaza at the intersection of Westminster and Weybosset Streets, stands one of the City's most recognizable buildings. This is true not only because of the unique shape of this 16-story high rise, but also because of the unique face that adorns its frieze.

Legend has it that on this site, once owned by Jacob Whitman, was his home and shop. In the mid-1700s, when Whitman roamed the land, it was customary for a shop owner to advertise with a catchy name or image to draw the attention of a relatively illiterate customer base. Whitman therefore mounted above his store, which he called "At the sign of the Turk's Head," a figure of an Ottoman warrior that, according to the legend, he retrieved from the ship *Sultan*.

• • •

149

Over 150 years later, the Brown family, subsequent owners of the property, hired the New York architectural firm of Howells & Strokes to design the current building as an investment. The 215 foot tall structure was completed in 1913 and though the original figurehead was no longer available the architects decided to incorporate into their design a Turk's Head sculpted out of granite. The sullen face can be seen overlooking the plaza from its 3rd-story perch over the center doors of the building.

Chapter 12

Rhode Island Convention Center

1 Sabin Street

BEARING FIGURE

Howard Ben Tre's columnar abstract is composed of bronze metal and green tinted glass. The Bearing Figure creates an abstracted human form giving the work a statue-like appearance. (Photo by Heather Caranci)

The Rhode Island Convention Center, built in 1996, is relatively modern by architectural standards and the sculpture located on the plaza at the entrance to the Center reflects that modernity. The sculpture is the work of Howard Ben Tre and was commissioned by the Rhode Island State Council on the Arts using funds from the state's One Percent for Art Program which requires that at least 1% of construction costs be appropriated for the inclusion of artwork.

The structure is a columnar abstract composed of bronze metal and green-tinted glass. It rests on a granite base and was installed on May 1, 1996. The sculpture creates an abstracted human form giving the work a statue-like appearance not readily apparent in most abstract works of art. The sculpture blends harmoniously with its surroundings whether viewed at eye level from the street or from above peering down from the windows of the convention center that it appears to stand guard over.

Chapter 13

Prince Hall Masonic Lodge

883 Eddy Street

HAND OF LIBERTY

Though standing in commemoration of Prince Hall's 18ᵗʰ and 19ᵗʰ century work in the establishment of the first Masonic Lodge devoted to African Americans, The Hand of Liberty may have actually been produced as part of a fundraising plan to raise money for the construction of Statue of Liberty. (Photo by Paul Caranci)

The birth of Prince Hall is shrouded in mystery. Legend has it that he was born in the mid-eighteenth century, perhaps as early as 1735, in the British West Indies to an English father and a black woman of French extraction. In about 1765, he worked passage onto a ship to Boston and apprenticed for his father learning the leather trade. Within eight years he is rumored to have acquired property and earn his right to vote. A man of faith, Hall became a minister in the African Methodist Episcopal Church in Cambridge at the age of 27 and married an enslaved woman. Eight years after her death Hall married Flora Gibbs of Gloucester, MA.

The accuracy of this legend is suspect but what is clear is that Hall became interested in Freemasonry and was rejected for membership upon his initial application into Boston's St. John's Lodge. Though rejected by colonial Freemasonry, Hall did not give up. Rather, he and 15 other black men applied for acceptance into a Boston group attached to British forces and were initiated into Lodge 441 of the Grand Lodge of Ireland on March 6, 1775. Sometime later, Hall and other freed men founded African Lodge No. 1 to which Hall was named Grand Master. The Lodge was later renamed African Lodge No 459 but because it had very limited powers Hall sought a separate charter from the Grand Lodge of England. The charter was granted allowing Hall and his members to build a new "African" movement on the foundation that existed as Masonry. On June 25, 1797, Hall organized African Lodge in Providence, RI which later changed its name to Hiram Lodge #3.

Hall died on December 4, 1807 but the family of Lodges he founded survive today with over 4,500 lodges and over 300,000 masons worldwide. The Providence Lodge is located at 883 Eddy Street. Proudly displayed between the building and the street is a light fixture sculpture known simply as the Hand of Liberty. A tall, narrow granite base is topped with a metal hand holding a torch of liberty which is actually an electric light fixture. Because the piece was on the property when the Masonic Lodge located there, not much is known about its origins. It has been suggested however that the torch may reference

• • •

the torch held by New York's Lady Liberty since her hand and torch were used throughout the United States in the 1880s to raise funds for the full monument. At a later date, a bronze plaque was added to the front of the granite base commemorating the role of Prince Hall for the establishment of the Lodge.

Chapter 14

Providence Public Library

225 Washington Street

TERPSICHORE

Terpsichore, the daughter of Zeus and Mnemosyn, and one of the nine muses described in Greek mythology, seems to stand guard in protection of the staircase at the Providence Public Library. (Photo by Paul Caranci)

Positioned on a landing as if guarding the upper hallway of the historic Providence Public Library stands a full-length bronze statue of Terpsichore, the Greek Muse of dancing and choral song. One of the nine Muses described in Greek religion, Terpsichore, the Goddess of lyric poetry and dancing whose name means "she who rejoices in the dance," is the daughter of Zeus and Mnemosyn. The other muses are Clio, Euterpe, Thalia, Melpomeni, Erato, Polymnia, Ourania and Calliope. So important were the Muses to the ancient writers that all generally begin their work with an appeal to the Muses. In both the Illiad and the Odyssey for example, Homer asks the Muses to tell the story in the most proper way. Even to modern day, the Muses remain symbols of inspiration and artistic creation.

Seen playing the flute in some versions, Terpsichore is perhaps the most widely known of the Muses. In some accounts she was the mother of the half-bird, half-woman Sirens, whose father was the sea god Achelous or the river god Phorcys.

The statue at the Providence Public Library was cast in Paris by Barbedienne, a 19th century metal worker and manufacturer, and was a memorial gift to the Library in 1921 by William Binney, Jr. in honor of his wife Harriet D'Costa Binney.

Binney is lineal descendent to one of the oldest families dating to the Colonial period. William Sr. was a Providence lawyer and the founder of the RI Hospital Trust Company. He was also the president of the City Council, author of the present city charter and a Providence legislator. William Jr. graduated Harvard in 1881and worked in the banking industry, first with his father at RI Hospital Trust Company, and later as a partner in the well-known firm, William Slade & company, bankers and brokers. Binney and his wife made their home on Providence's East Side at 72 Prospect Street.

The Providence version of Terpsichore is a rather unusual casting as it is a full-length standing statue. Most images of the Muse depict her holding a lyre and plectrum, but in a sitting position.

Section III

The Neighborhoods

Chapter 15

Fox Point

George M. Cohan Plaza
Wickenden Street

GEORGE M. COHAN

*George M. Cohan has been described as the greatest song and dance man in Broadway history.
The composer of Over There, one of the most popular patriotic songs of all time, is honored with
this bronze monument on the site of his birth in Fox Point. (Photo by Paul Caranci)*

• • •

George M. Cohan was born in Providence, Rhode Island on July 3, 1878. At an early age, Cohan, whose Irish Catholic parents were in show business, performed in vaudeville as well as on the "legitimate stage." One of his first rolls was a musical comedy called The Four Cohans in which he starred with his sister and parents. While still a youth, Cohan also began to write songs and plays.

His first New York debut, a play he wrote in 1901 called *The Governor's Son*, was far from a classic. His second attempt, however, a play written in 1904 called *Little Johnny Jones* began a string of stage and music successes that included such great song titles as *Over There* and *You're a Grand Old Flag* which have since become American standards.

On October 19, 1941, Cohan received a Congressional Medal of Honor from President Franklin D. Roosevelt for writing *Over There* and in 1942, *Yankee Doodle Dandy*, a classic movie about Cohan's life, earned James Cagney an academy award for his portrayal of songwriting genius.

After a one-year illness, Cohan died at 5:00 in the morning of November 6, 1942 having given his country the greatest song of World War I. He died surrounded by family and closest friends in his New York home overlooking Central Park. Today he is considered one of the greatest, if not THE greatest song and dance man in Broadway history. All but eight of his sixty-four years were devoted to the stage.

Though he was famous for songs and dances in many productions, it was as the author of *Over There* that earned Cohan international respect. America had not seen such a popular patriotic song since the Civil War.

In 2009, Sculptor Robert Shure was commissioned to create a statue of Cohan which now marks the site of his Wickenden Street birthplace. The bronze bust was cast by Skylight Studios, Inc and is mounted on a stone pedestal. The statue depicts Cohan from the waist up clothed in a buttoned vest and suit jacket with a bow tie around his neck. The upper torso is in full dance pose with a top derby hat raised about head high in his right hand. Dedications ceremonies were held on July 3, 2009 and featured a parade, music and speeches from the newly renamed George M. Cohan Plaza. Transplanted New Yorkers, Sy and Judi Dill, spearheaded the effort to build the statue in Providence.

Chapter 16

Federal Hill

Msgr. Cavallaro Plaza
Corner of Dean Street and Atwells Avenue

REVEREND MONSIGNOR
GALLIANO J. CAVALLARO

A long-time pastor of Our Lady of Mount Carmel Church on Federal Hill, the Reverend Monsignor Galliano J. Cavallaro was honored with a bronze bust in a plaza that bears his name. The bust is located in Cavallaro Plaza at the north-west corner of Atwells Avenue and Dean Street. (Photo by Heather Caranci)

● ● ●

When Angelina Tomassi Cavallaro blessed her husband Giueseppe with their son Galliano, they had no way of knowing that life's path would lead him from Federal Hill to the priesthood, but after completing a Catholic education that included LaSalle Academy High School, St. Charles College in Maryland and St. Mary's Seminary in Baltimore he was ordained a priest by Bishop Francis Keough at the Cathedral of St. Peter & Paul on December 19, 1942. He celebrated his first Mass at Our Lady of Mount Carmel, his boyhood parish and, in 1960, after serving at a number of parishes, Cavallaro was named Pastor of the very church he once served as an alter boy. In 1967 Pope Paul VI named him an Honorary Prelate of His Holiness with the title of Right Reverend Monsignor.

Serving as the Director of Diocesan Catholic Cemeteries for 40 years, Cavallaro revolutionized the burial grounds earning similar positions in secular organizations and recognition as a national expert while presiding over the opening of three new Catholic cemeteries in his home state. He also served for many years as diocesan chaplain to Italian immigrants and the diocese representative to Italian-speaking civic organizations.

His 1974 vision to beautify the area in front of Mt. Carmel Church helped stimulate the revitalization of Federal Hill. On January 26, 1979 the resulting plaza at the corner of Atwells Avenue and Dean Street was named in his honor with the centerpiece becoming a statue in his likeness dedicated on October 21st of that year by Bishop Louis E. Gelineau. The stone bust stands on a granite column base and was done by an unidentified sculptor. The bust can be found on the corner of Dean Street approaching Atwells Avenue.

Though he retired in 2000 at the age of 85, Cavallaro continued to assist many parishes until his passing at the age of 95 on March 7, 2010.

Chapter 17

The West End

310 Cranston Street

EBENEZER KNIGHT DEXTER

Described in 1894 by RI Supreme Court Chief Justice Thomas Durfee as a munificent public benefactor, Ebenezer Knight Dexter bequeathed to Providence a significant amount of land that includes the site of the Cranston Street Armory and the Brown University Athletic Complex, originally the 40-acre site of the Dexter Asylum, a facility for the town's poor. (Photo by Paul Caranci)

● ● ●

"In the swirling, swiftly flowing current of our complex civilization, men are inclined to neglect, if not to disregard the lessons which have been drawn from the experiences of human kind. It is profitable, therefore, to pause now and then, amid the engrossing activities of a busy life, and take a retrospective view of past events, that our minds may be so enlightened thereby that our future action shall be guided by wisdom and prudence." With those words, spoken on June 29, 1894, 120 years ago, Acting Providence Mayor Daniel R. Ballou, unveiled the statue commemorating the life, generosity and philanthropy of Ebenezer Knight Dexter.

The handsome bronze figure, located in the heart of the Dexter Training Grounds, is 8 feet tall and stands upon a magnificent granite pedestal that is nine feet high. Mr. Dexter is represented in continental costume; in his left hand is a walking stick and in his right, a partially opened scroll of parchment. The inscription on the pedestal, which was designed by Parks Commissioner R. H. Deming, reads, *"Presented to the citizens of Providence by Henry C. Clark, Esq., in honor of Ebenezer Knight Dexter, who gave his property for the benefit of the public and the homeless, 1893."* The other side of the pedestal is inscribed, *"Leaving nothing but a headstone to mark our passage through life does not make the world better. They live best who serve humanity the most."*

By all accounts of those present at the dedication, a contingent that numbered nearly 1,000 dignitaries, citizens and students standing beneath the low grey clouds responsible for the steady drizzle that fell upon them, these words epitomized the life of Ebenezer Knight Dexter. Unlike Abraham Lincoln, Oliver Hazard Perry, Nathanael Greene, Ezek Hopkins and so many others honored in statue however, nary a person today seems to know who Dexter was or why his life warranted such warm and honored remembrance.

A descendant in the sixth generation of Roger Williams' dear and faithful friend, Gregory Dexter, Ebenezer Knight Dexter was born on April 26, 1773, a year before disgruntled Rhode Island colonists burned the HMS Gaspee and three years before the signing of the Declaration of Independence. He was just nine when peace was declared following the Revolution and though too young to fully grasp the significance of what he had seen and heard, he was surely old enough to "catch the spirit of his elders and their spirited devotion"

● ● ●

prompted by the horrors of those wartime events. That had to have had a profound influence on his life.

He is presumed to have been beneficiary of a sound education and embarked on a career in business following the adoption of the Federal Constitution, and the "rising tide of prosperous trade and commerce" that followed it. He approached his business with such devotion that he was able to retire with a fortune when most men his age were just starting to think about accumulating one. He was appointed United States Marshall for the District of Rhode Island in 1810, a position he would hold until his untimely death at age 51. Though financially sound and well respected, his life was full of the same difficulties that many others were also forced to endure. Having already suffered the loss of his only child, Mary, just five months and ten days after her birth, Dexter suffered a heavy affliction in the death of his only true love, his wife Waitstill, in 1819.

Upon his own death on August 10, 1824, The Providence Gazette wrote, "...In all the relations in his life he was a man of exemplary morals. As a son, brother, and a husband, dutiful, affectionate and liberal; prompt and conscientious in the discharge of his official duties, scrupulous and just in his dealings, and attached by principle to the institutions and liberties of his country, his death is a subject of regret to a numerous circle of relatives and friends, to his neighbors and fellow citizens and to the public institutions of which he was an active and efficient member..."

The reading of his will, according to Retired Chief Justice Thomas Durfee, "exhibited him [Dexter] in a new, and, in some respects, nobler aspect, as a munificent public benefactor." Dexter left much of his property to the City of Providence. Two of the larger tracts, The Dexter Training Ground, on which stands his statue, and the Dexter Asylum, a 40 acre parcel on Providence's East Side (now the site of the Brown University Athletic Complex) on which was constructed the Dexter Asylum for the use and accommodation of the poor of the town.

Dexter was driven to philanthropy by a deep rooted sense of public spirit and benevolence, "a strong attachment," he declared in his will, "to my native town and an ardent desire to ameliorate the condition of the poor and contribute to their comfort and relief."

• • •

These, according to Durfee, are two of the purest and loftiest of human motives. Every expression which I have seen, coming from his contemporaries, is confirmatory of the sincerity of his declaration."

Chapter 18

The North End

480 Branch Avenue

ESEK HOPKINS

He was both a hero and a villain all at the same time, but Esek Hopkins played a significant role in the continental Navy's successes that aided the colonist's cause in the American Revolution. The first Commander of the Continental Navy retired to a life of community service to his hometown of North Providence. (Photo courtesy of the Rhode Island State Archives, Preston Collection, C#858

When Esek Hopkins was chosen to command the Continental Navy it was a fledgling armada in need of a gregarious leader. Hopkins was up to the challenge!

Born on April 26, 1718 in Chapumiscook, Rhode Island, the modern day Scituate, Esek was one of nine children. His early years, like those of his siblings, were spent sharing the work on the farm of his parents William and Ruth. Shortly after the 1738 death of his father, however, Esek ventured to Providence to become a sailor. Esek had long dreamed of the allure of the sea and the potential rewards of life as a privateer and now found the reality to be most provocative.

• • •

Just three years after leaving home he had become a prominent master mariner. He would later write that privateering was "Rhode Island's most profitable enterprise during the years before the American Revolutionary War."

While in port in 1743, the tall, good looking Hopkins fell in love with and married Desire Burroughs, the daughter of a Newport deacon. They set up residence in Newport where Esek continued to sail as a privateer during the King George's and the French and Indian Wars enhancing his skills and accumulating significant wealth. When the wars had finally ended in 1763, the 45-year old Hopkins had become sea weary and decided to become an entrepreneur, opening a business with his older brother Stephen and moving his family to North Providence. He also continued to sail for John Brown and his brothers from the Port of Providence, and was captain of the Sally, Brown's slave ship that carried almost 140 slaves to their death.

With growing discontent of British leadership, however, thoughts of revolution began to circulate. There is even speculation that Hopkins may have been an active participant in the colonist burning of the *HMS Gaspee* on June 9, 1772, an event that precipitated the Revolution. Regardless of his participation in the Gaspee affair, the Rhode Island Legislature asked Hopkins to serve as the overall commander of the colony's militia, conferring upon him the rank of brigadier general in May 1773.

His brother Stephen, meanwhile, was totally immersed in the Continental Congress's efforts to seek independence. As one of Rhode Island's delegates he used his clout to convince Congress to commission a navy of the united colonies, arming 13 vessels for that purpose. He also insisted on his brother Esek's appointment as the new Navy's commander-in-chief. The Continental Congress obliged with an appointment on November 5, 1775.

Just two months later Congress instructed Esek to proceed directly to the Chesapeake Bay in Virginia. Though issuing a very specific charge, Hopkins disobeyed, opting instead to sail to the Port of New Providence in the Bahamas. There, he undertook a most ambitious, and the first amphibious, offensive. On March 3rd, Hopkins landed his marines and sailors who seized the local British defensive works, taking munitions desperately needed for the colonist's war efforts toward independence.

· · ·

On his return to Rhode Island he also captured and took command of two British merchantmen and one six-gun schooner. On April 4th, Hopkins encountered and took command of two more British warships; The *Hawk*, an armed schooner and the bomb brig *Bolton*. His reputation was now exploding and thoughts of his lack of attention to a direct command were beginning to wane. That is until April 6th. On that day, with his crew tired and overworked, some suffering from an outbreak of fevers and smallpox and others manning the captured ships, Hopkins encountered the British Sloop Glasgow, a 20-gun frigate under the command of Tryingham Howe and decided to engage. The guns of the frigate caused significant damage to three of Hopkins' ships, killing ten of his men and wounding 14 others. Hopkins was forced to flee to New London to unload some captured tender and suffering from a most humiliating defeat.

Upon his return, the likes of John Hancock and John Adams rose to his defense citing his heroics, but too many others found opportunity for criticism. Congress censured Hopkins for violating orders by sailing to Nassau rather than Virginia and for unloading captured tender without approval. He was dismissed from the Navy in January 1778 and his command was handed to his protégé, John Paul Jones.

Now 60, Hopkins returned to his North Providence farm to a hero's welcome. For much of the next decade he served as an elected member of the Rhode Island General Assembly. He died at home on February 26, 1802 at the age of 82 and was buried in a family burial ground in Providence.

Hopkins efforts and naval accomplishments provided a vital boost to the war effort. Despite the abrupt ending to his career, the capture of the British fort in the Bahamas was crucial in disrupting the British war effort in the American colonies. It deprived the British of a key point in their trade route and provided a port that served a pivotal role in the naval conflicts between Britain and France.

In 1891, the Providence City Council exercised it powers of eminent domain by taking the Hopkins family burial ground in the City's North End at the corner of Charles Street and Branch Avenue for public purposes. All of the graves, save Esek's, were relocated to the North Burial Ground and plans were begun for a park and monument in Hopkins' honor. Sculptor Theodora Alice Ruggles Kitson, the wife of renowned sculptor Henry Kitson (sculptor of the Thomas Doyle statue and the Falconer) was commissioned to create the full length standing bronze figure. Set atop a high granite base, the Admiral is pointing toward the horizon with his right hand which also grasps a compass. Harriette Coggeshall, a descendent of Hopkins, bequeathed to the City the $3,250 required for production of the statue which was cast by the Gorham Company.

Chapter 19

Downtown

The Historic District is listed on the National Register of Historic Places

THE HIKER

The Hiker, originally called The Spirit of '96, has "presided over" at least three major renovations of Kennedy Plaza since its dedication in 1911. The larger-than-life bronze statue commemorates the American Army and Navy involvement in the Spanish American War of 1898. (Photo by Heather Caranci)

● ● ●

Located on Memorial Square, the island resting between Providence City Hall and the John O. Pastore Federal Building, stands a replica of a statue created in 1906 by Theodora Alice Ruggles Kitson and commissioned by the National Association of Spanish War Veterans. *The Hiker*, originally titled *The Spirit of '96*, was a gift of the Rhode Island Chapter of the national organization and represents a common practice of such groups to commission replicas of famous statues for local use. In this instance, the Gorham Company purchased the design of the statue from Kitson and cast it several times. The designer was paid a royalty as each casting was sold. Gorham continued to cast this particular figure for decades and sold well over 50 that are installed in various towns across the country. Kitson's original work is located in Minnesota. Other replicas of this statue, for example, are located in Fall River, Massachusetts and in Washington, DC.

This bronze replica depicts a typical infantryman standing upon a boulder and clutching a rifle with both hands in a resting position, the rifle is horizontal in front of him. He is dressed for tropical warfare, his shirt open at the collar and his sleeves rolled up. He is wearing a broad-brimmed hat for protection against the sun. With an ammunition belt wrapped around his waist he appears ready for action.

The boulder on which he stands presents a bronze plaque with a bas-relief that represents the American Army and Navy aiding the rebellious Spanish colonies.

It was bestowed upon the City of Providence in 1911 and was originally intended for dedication at the North Burial Ground. The change of heart may be representative of two separate phenomena of the time; a determined desire to memorialize veterans of the Spanish American War, the Philippine Insurrection, and the China relief expedition in a fashion afforded to the veterans of other wars, and a simultaneous loss of interest in funerary markers.

SOLDIERS AND SAILORS MONUMENT

Designed by Randolph Rogers in 1866, the Soldiers and Sailors Monument cost $60,000. It features America, a 10' tall bronze standing female figure, perched atop a multi-tiered monument that has four additional bronze figures a tier below representing the infantry, artillery, cavalry and navy involvement in the Civil War. Cannon and cannon ball adorn the steps of the lower tier. (Post card from the author's collection)

In the years following the Civil War a plethora of monuments were erected all over the country to its commemoration. The Providence version was designed by Randolph Rogers in 1866, cost $60,000 and was dedicated on September 16, 1871 in front of Harrington Opera House, where City Hall now stands. From her perch 40 feet above the ground, a bronze standing figure of a classically draped America extends a laurel wreath from her right hand while holding a wreath of immortelles with her left.

Below the 10' figure of America, on perches of blue Westerly granite, stand four additional bronze statues each bearing the attributes and weapons of the branch of service he represents; infantry, artillery cavalry and navy. Below each military statue is a bronze honor roll listing the state's war dead. The honor rolls alternate with relief panels depicting portrayals of War, Victory, Peace and History.

One tier lower, four cannon rest on individual granite platforms, while one tier below that rest eight mounds of cannon balls, two mounds beneath each cannon. The cannon and cannon balls are separated by four sets of granite steps that lead from the ground to the base on which the military statues stand.

On the relief panel called History is one of the earliest representations of an African-American in the history of American sculpture. It depicts a black figure in classical dress about knee length and exhibits the broken shackles of emancipation.

The monument was sculpted in Rome, moved to Munich and assembled in Providence by the architect. In 1913 the monument, which is among Rhode Island's most elaborate and beautiful, was relocated to the center of Kennedy Plaza where it underwent restoration in 1992. It was relocated to its original and current location in 1997 as part of the renovations to the plaza.

THOMAS A. DOYLE

During his 18 plus years as Mayor of Providence Thomas A. Doyle administered what is arguably the greatest period of development in City history. Providence more than doubled in population and wealth and a significant number of improvements were made including the installation of a sewer system, and the advent of a professional, trained police department. (Photo courtesy of the Rhode Island State Archives, Preston Collection, C#858)

Thomas A. Doyle presided over the City of Providence as the 9th, 11th and 13th Mayor. His time in office covered from June 1864 to June 1869, again from June 1870 to June 1881 and finally from January 1884 until his death on June 9, 1886. He died at the age of 59, making him at the time only the 2nd Mayor of Providence to die during his term of office. He administered a period of significant growth and arguably the greatest period of development in City history. During his 18 plus years in office, the City more than doubled in population and wealth and a number of significant improvements were made. City Hall was constructed, a highly acclaimed sewerage system was adopted, Roger Williams Park was developed, many

● ● ●

public buildings were erected and the police department was molded into a professional, trained force. He was the longest serving mayor in the City at the time of his death and his record was eclipsed only by Mayor Vincent Cianci who served a total of just over 21 years.

The statue is a bronze figure of Doyle standing with his left hand on his hip and the other clutching a rolled plan. He is wearing a nineteenth century frock coat and sports the dramatic whiskers for which he was known making the likeness very realistic. The full-length standing portrait rests atop a tall rectangular base. It was commissioned shortly after Doyle's death as a testament to his popularity in the City. The selected artist was the well-known sculptor Henry Hudson Kitson who, though creating a number of Civil War memorials was best known for his statue of The Minute Man in Lexington, Massachusetts. Kitson was born in Boston, MA, but trained in Paris where he also had the bronze statue of Doyle cast.

The Doyle statue was dedicated in 1889 and placed in front of the Catholic Cathedral of Saints Peter and Paul. During the extensive renovations of Weybossett Hill in 1967, the statue was repositioned at its present location at the corner of Broad and Chestnut Streets. The inscription on the statue's stone base reads, *"Thomas A. Doyle"* *"Eighteen Years Mayor of Providence"* *"Pioneer in Urban Renewal."*

IRISH FAMINE MEMORIAL

In the mid 19ᵗʰ century, 1.5 million people fled Ireland in hopes of finding a better life. Many came to America. The Irish Famine Memorial, built along the Providence Riverwalk, has multiple components. The Commemorative Wall, pictured here, is inscribed with the history of the famine amid the Irish immigration. The sidewalk below the wall illustrates a map of the coasts of Ireland and America. (Photo by Heather Caranci)

Between the years 1845 and 1851, Ireland, then still a colony of England, was hit with a great famine. The famine had a devastating effect on the Irish citizens and was part of the impetus that spurred a massive emigration of the Irish to America and other parts of the world. In all, about 1.5 million people fled Ireland in the hopes of finding a better life.

In October in the year of the 150ᵗʰ anniversary of the start of The Great Famine, a Mass was held in the Roman Catholic Cathedral of Saints Peter and Paul in the capital city. Out of that solemn commemorative event was born the idea of the creation of the state's first Irish Famine Memorial.

● ● ●

In May 1997, a memorial committee was formed and commissioned Robert Shure to design a permanent, tasteful monument to venerate the one million victims of Ireland's Great Famine. On November 17, 2007, the completed monument was dedicated along the Riverwalk in downtown Providence and serves as a powerful and lasting tribute to the sufferings and triumphs of those impacted by The Great Famine. The monument maintains the memory and historical meaning of the event for future generations of any ethnic or cultural background.

The multi-component memorial consists of three larger-than-life statues of Irish figures mounted on a stone base. A woman, sitting in a mournful position cradling the limp body of a loved one whose life was ended by hunger, faces toward the world left behind in Ireland and memorializes the suffering of the Irish people during the famine years. A third figure in full stride, with a coat thrown over his left arm, bravely walks in the other direction symbolizing the start of a new life in the land of plenty. The sculpture, therefore, unites the despair of their past with an enduring sense of optimism for their lives in a new land. The figures were cast in bronze by Skylight Studios, Inc. of Massachusetts.

A walkway leads from the statue to a commemorative wall on which is inscribed the history of the famine amid the Irish immigration. The sidewalk beneath the wall illustrates a map of the coasts of Ireland and America and emphasizes the audacious journey of the Irish people to the United States.

Dr. Donald D. Deignan chairs the Commission that continues its fundraising efforts to provide adequate funding for the long-term maintenance of the memorial. Donations may be made through the website at http://www.rifaminememorial.org/

The main component of the Irish Famine Memorial is this larger-than-life bronze statue designed by Robert Shure and dedicated on November 17, 2007. A woman cradles the lifeless body of a loved one who has succumbed to starvation. A third figure walks toward a better life in a land of opportunity. (Photo by Heather Caranci)

TEXTURAL GEAR

Textural Gear is the eye catching design of Massachusetts sculptor Rob Lorenson. Located along the Providence Riverwalk, the sculpture was first displayed in Rhode Island at the 2001 Convergence International Arts Festival. (Photo by Paul Caranci)

It's been described as an oversized silver truck tire, a silver circle and an angry donut. Indeed, it resembles all three. In reality, this work of art along the City's Riverwalk is called Textural Gear. It is the 1997 creation of Massachusetts sculptor Rob Lorenson who built it in Dekalb, Illinois, just outside of Chicago. A similar piece was built for the Navy Pier show in Chicago earlier and, because Lorenson hadn't completed his mental vision of that work, he decided to design this piece which he displayed in the 2001 Convergence International Arts Festival held in Providence. "I had pretty much grown to love stainless steel as a medium," Lorenson said in an interview. "One of the things I like most about it was how surfaces, when worked with a scotch brite pad, reflected the local colors." The Riverwalk location

• • •

could not be better for this purpose as the Textural Gear uses the color of the sky, the water, the concrete and the nearby grass to attract the viewer's eye.

The gear teeth are from the Navy Pier work and came from industrial areas in Chicago. This piece forms a natural contrast to Lorenson's previous work which is more futuristic. Lorenson feels the "two treatments are opposites yet united by their common material" and finds the balance that is maintained between them quite appealing.

The artist noted that Textural Gear's location nicely frames the old factory building across the river "representing and reliving what they were a generation ago. It also tells a tale that we are currently living of rebirth of industrial America through innovation."

Lorneson's work is featured in over 200 public and private collections.

PROVIDENCE VETERANS MEMORIAL

Mayor Vincent Cianci fittingly chose Veterans Day, Novem-

The Providence Veterans Memorial is located at 15 LaSalle Square just outside of the Hasbro, Inc., where some 300 of its domestic sales, marketing, packaging and global operations workers are employed. The memorial is across from the Dunkin Donuts Center and includes a memorial stone for various wars including World War II, Korea and Vietnam, on which are inscribed the names of the fallen. (Photo by Heather Caranci)

ber 11, 1981, to dedicate the City's memorial to the fallen servicemen and women of World War II, Korea and Vietnam. Situated at 15 LaSalle Square along Hasbro place at the convergence of Empire, Fountain and Sabin Streets is a large monument that consists of 12 granite stones, 8 granite benches, 3 poles displaying the flags of the United States, Rhode Island and Providence, and a large circular granite planter all surrounded by a concrete and brick plaza outside of the Hasbro, Inc. administration building.

The first stone tells the story of the monument while nine stones list the war dead of World War II. There is one stone listing those who gave their lives in Korea and another for those who perished in Vietnam. The memorial stones are linked by a steel design though separated into two groups with a center divide. Each individual stone is inscribed at its base with a single word "Honor," "Courage," "Duty," "Loyalty," "Country," and "Heroism." This word pattern repeats on either side of the center divide.

Chapter 20

East Side

251 Benefit Street

RICHMOND FOUNTAIN

The historic Providence Athanaeum at 251 Benefit Street was chartered in 1836. It wasn't until a year later, however, that the equally historic gothic style Richmond Fountain was built. This design of Ware and Van Brunt was the gift of Anna Richmond. (Photo by Paul Caranci)

• • •

Standing in front of the historic Providence Athanaeum at 251 Benefit Street is a most impressive gothic style fountain of historic significance equal to that of the Athenaeum itself. The Athenaeum was chartered in 1836 and the fountain was built a year later. Designed by Ware and Van Brunt, an architectural firm out of Boston, this gift of Anna Richmond contains a drinking basin carved into a ten feet high retaining wall. Four columns of polished Quincy granite support a molded arch in which are inscribed the words, "Come hither everyone that thirsteth." The bases of the columns are sculpted from white Concord granite. A shell-like basin is filled with water pouring from a spigot above and subsequently overflowing into a second, larger basin at ground level. Although legend has it that "everyone who drinks the water are sure to return," the water today is not a suitably potable supply.[17]

[17] The Providence Athenaeum's Athenaeum Omniumgatherum Fascinating Facts
http://www.providenceathenaeum.org/facts/facts.html

• • •

Chapter 21

Silver Lake

Silver Lake Avenue
(Moorfield Street)

BLESSED SCALABRINI

The bust of Blessed Giovanni Scalabrini, the founder of the Congregation of Missionaries of St. Charles, now known as the Scalabrinian Fathers and Brothers, is located on the original site of St. Bartholomew's Church. The church's original bell tower and the bust are now the focal points of Scalabrini Piazza. (Photo by Heather Caranci)

● ● ●

Twenty four years after Giovanni Battista Scalabrini was ordained into the Catholic priesthood Bishop Scalabrini founded the Congregation of the Missionaries of St. Charles, since known as the Scalabrinian Fathers and Brothers. The initial mission of the order was to "maintain Catholic faith and practice among Italian emigrants in the New World." Over the ensuing years they, and their three sister organizations, also founded by Scalabrini, expanded their mission to include ministries to seafarers, refugees and displaced persons in addition to the migrants they originally intended to serve.

While largely Hispanic today, the Providence neighborhood of Silver Lake on the city's western border was traditionally an Italian-American settlement dating from the mid-19th century and continuing through to the 1990s when nearly 43% of Silver Lake residents claimed at least some Italian ancestry. In 1907 the Diocese of Providence approved the construction of St. Bartholomew's Church on Silver Lake Avenue (Moorefield Street) to serve the spiritual needs of many of those residents. The Parish is staffed by the Missionary Fathers of St. Charles Borromeo (Congregation of Scalabrinians - C.S.) and the Rev. Leonardo Quaglia, was named the first pastor of the independent parish.

So important was this Church to the Italian community that when the church relocated to Laurel Hill about 1/3 mile away in 1969, the bell tower was left standing as a monument to the original site of the Church. The area was renamed Scalabrini Piazza and the statue of Blessed Scalabrini was placed in his honor.

Chapter 22

South Providence

239 Oxford Street

ST. MICHAEL THE ARCHANGEL

Among the seven Archangels of Roman Catholic tradition, St. Michael the Archangel is considered an Archangel in Jewish, Christian and Islamic teachings. On September 29, 1953, the children, both past and present, of St. Michael's School donated the statue of their patron as a centennial gift to their parish. (Photo by Paul Caranci)

Ranked among the seven Archangels of Roman Catholic tradition is St. Michael. In fact, St. Michael is one of only three (the others are St. Raphael and St. Gabriel) Archangels mentioned in the Bible. With two references in the Old Testament and two in the New, St. Michael is considered an Archangel in Jewish, Christian and Islamic teachings. It is Michael who is sent in a vision to comfort Daniel and it is he who is represented as the great support of Israel during the seventy years of the Babylonian captivity. He is referred to as "The Great Prince who sendeth for the children of Thy people."[18]

It may have been with this in mind that the emerging Irish immigrant population of Providence's south side rallied around the construction of the new church bearing St. Michael's name. The nearly twenty-five year construction project was designed by Murhpy, Hindle and Wright in the Anglo-Norman gothic style. The Church is the focal point of an architecturally harmonious group of buildings. It is flanked by a convent, a school and a rectory, all of which were added to the National Register of Historic Places. It remains today the largest minority parish in Providence.

On September 29, 1953, the children, both past and present, of St. Michael's School donated the statue of their patron as a centennial gift to their parish. The standing concrete statue depicts the Archangel as the defender of the faithful. His right hand points the tip of his sword at an unchained dragon, symbolizing the conquest of evil. The beast is held down in defeat by the right foot of St. Michael. The statue is mounted on a concrete base faced with stones.

On June 9, 2002, the statue was rededicated in commemoration of the 25th anniversary of the November 6, 1976 ordination of parish priest, Rev. Raymond B. Malm.

---

[18] from the Bible – Daniel XII

Section IV

Parks

Chapter 23

Roger Williams Park

1000 Elmwood Avenue

THE SENTINEL

The Sentinel has been a favorite statue of visitors of Roger Williams Park for generations. The bronze of this heroic mastiff is perhaps the most photographed sculpture in the Park. (Photo by Heather Caranci)

The Hoppin family of Providence was widely considered one of the most pre-eminent mid-nineteenth century artistic families in the country with many of its members prominent in the arts community. Thomas Frederick Hoppin was a particularly successful painter, but it was his sculpture of a dog that turned out to be the most popular of all his works. Why a dog, in fact, why *this* dog turns out to be a very interesting story itself.

John Inness Clark lived with his family in a three story wood mansion at 357 Benefit Street at the corner of John Street on the City's very affluent and historic East Side. Subsequent to his death, his widow Lydia sold the "Mansion House" to William Almy who married Sarah Brown, the daughter of Moses Brown. The couple's daughter Anna married successful industrialist William Jenkins becoming the richest woman in America.

On the quiet, chilly evening of November 20, 1849, while the family slept, a fire ravaged the house. Black Prince, the large Mastiff owned by the Jenkins family, broke free of his chain and barked loudly waking 17 year old Anna and her 15 year old brother Moses saving them from the ravages of the inferno. They were the only two survivors of the dreaded night as Mrs. Jenkins and her youngest daughter perished in the blaze.

Shortly after the fire, sometime between 1849 and 1861, Anna married Thomas F. Hoppin who, with his family, lived on Westminster Street at the corner of Walnut St at the western edge of the City. Thomas, the ninth in line of twelve children had already established himself as a remarkable and talented artist. He was described as an opulent man with exquisitely fitted cloths who wore a tall beaver hat and a monocle in his left eye. He carried a cane, wore gloves and frequently had a greyhound at his side.[19] In 1861, he and Anna moved into a house they had built around 1853 in place of the fire reduced Clark House that was built in 1791 and reportedly used to entertain President George Washington.

The Hoppin House, as it became known, was built by architect Alpheus C. Morse in the influence of Sir Charles Barry and in 1893 was described "as an example of the very best work in Italian Renaissance, a style in which Mr. Morse delighted to work."[20] The house alternately was called the "'House of 1,000 Candles' because of the lavish entertainment that went on there."

Though primarily a painter of spirited war and animal scenes, Hoppin felt compelled to memorialize the animal that saved his wife's life. He executed the striking bronze statue of the Mastiff in 1851 and had it cast by the Gorham Company. It is a 300 pound, life-size bronze of the massive, life-altering animal. This is actually the first outdoor sculpture in Rhode Island and one of the first bronze statues ever cast in the United States of America. Such a striking example it is that

---

[19] Historic American Buildings Survey, National Park Service, Eastern Office, Division of Design and Construction, 143 South Third St., Philadelphia 6, Pennsylvania – prepared by Antoinette F. Downing, Elvira Gowdey and Osmund R. Overby, Architect for the Providence Preservation Society, July 1961

[20] Obituary of Alpheus C. Morse from the Providence Journal, November 27, 1893

• • •

when it was shown at Crystal Palace in London, it won a gold medal from the New York Academy of Design. The bronze Mastiff wears a thick studded collar and has a chain draped over his back. The statue took a prominent position as a lawn sculpture in the front of the Benefit Street mansion where it stood until 1896 when the family donated it to the City of Providence.

It was placed in Roger Williams Park where it has taken up several positions including on Frederick C. Green Memorial Blvd. and in the Japanese Gardens. Today it stands at the Park Zoo, where, over the course of generations, it has become the Park's mascot and a favorite among visitors, especially the children, many of whom stop to take a photo perched on the large dog's back.

THE FALCONER

This striking depiction of a young athlete falconing was the gift of Daniel Wanton Lyman in memory of his maternal grandfather, Governor Elisha Dyer. The Falconer is pictured here in its original location on the island in Pleasure Lake, now home to the Japanese Garden. (Post card image from the author's collection)

Textile manufacturer Daniel Wanton Lyman had much to be thankful for. He was born of good stock, was provided a sound education and had been given the opportunity to accumulate great wealth and political influence. He made the most of those opportunities.

His paternal grandfather, Daniel Lyman, was born in 1756. After graduating from Yale he enlisted as a Major in the war for independence participating in some great battles of the American Revolution. After the war he married Mary "Poly" Wanton and the couple had 13 children. Daniel worked first as a surveyor in Newport, then as a lawyer where his skills were most obvious. In 1802 he accepted an appointment as Chief Justice of the Rhode Island Supreme Court, a position he held until his retirement in 1816. It was in retirement that he turned his attention to manufacturing. With partners he started the Lyman Cotton Manufacturing Company in North Providence where the mill village of Lymansville still bears the family name. Even in the manufacturing business, Lyman excelled and his mill became the first in the nation to build reservoirs upstream from the dam so as to have water available to feed the waterfalls that provided power to the mill so there would be no loss of production during the summer's dry months. His was also the first mill in America to employ the use of water-powered scotch looms in the manufacture of cotton, a process most other mills eventually copied. The successes of young Daniel's paternal grandfather, however, did not overshadow those of his maternal grandfather, Elisha Dyer.

Born in 1811, Elisha Dyer was successful in many of his life's endeavors. He excelled in business and as a musician. He was a banker and a railroad magnate, a world traveler, a philanthropist and, perhaps most importantly, a civic leader involved in too many boards and commissions to list. It was as a public servant, however, that Dyer may have made his most significant contributions. Dyer was elected state adjutant general of Rhode Island in 1840 as a member of the Law and Order government established during the Dorr Rebellion. He was elected Governor of the state in 1857 and again in 1858. He declined nomination for a third term. Upon leaving office, the Providence Post wrote, "We have from the first looked upon him as an honorable, highminded opponent and a straightforward conscientious man; and candor compels us to say that he has never failed to reach the standard set up for him."

It is no wonder that Henry Bull Lyman and Caroline Dyer Lyman, young Daniel's parents, inherited not only substantial wealth and political and social status, but a deep rooted desire to work hard and serve, traits they clearly passed to Daniel both during their lives and after. In fact, though never needing to work a day in his life, Daniel was eager to serve his country. During the early days of the Civil War when President Lincoln called upon RI Governor William Sprague to provide troops, Sprague turned to General Ambrose Burnside for leadership. Immediately responding to the call, he asked for volunteers to serve under him. Still in high school, Daniel Wanton Lyman led his classmates in the formation of The Ellsworth Phalanx. The group was named in honor of the youthful and lamented commander of the New York Zouaves, who was shot at Alexandria, VA on May 24, 1861 after tearing down a confederate flag that President Lincoln had pointed out. "I will lower that flag with my own hands," the boy said to Lincoln. "He had so much of the boy in him that he rushed forward and was shot," it was later recalled.

Leadership of the Ellsworth Phalanx was entrusted to Daniel Wanton Lyman who was elected Captain and worked to "realize his ambition to make 'the Corps' as he loved to call it, the best-drilled and equipped company in Rhode Island."[21]

Daniel returned from war and graduated Brown then turned to a life of philanthropy. It was not only service to his country that young Daniel cherished, but service to his state, community, friends and family as well. As was recalled by former Governor Elisha Dyer at the dedication of a Civil War monument bequeathed to his home town of North Providence and published in the 1913 publication of *Daniel Wanton Lyman 1844 – 1886 An Appreciation*, "The crowning glory of his life after all was the tender and devoted affection for his mother. From early womanhood, by reason of accident, she had been permanently lame, and nothing that he could do to promote her comfort or her happiness was neglected. Neither the claims of business nor the attractions of society kept him from his watchful care of his mother. To be with her and to minister to her every want and help her bear the burdens of age and sickness, was the absorbing desire of his heart and stands out pre-eminent as a beautiful trait in his character."

Daniel Wanton Lyman died a most untimely death at the age of just 42 after spending all his post war years trying to improve the lives of others and pushing them to excellence. Even in death he continued that effort. Virtually all his fortune was left to charity not forgetting the family he so loved. Lyman bequeathed the funds necessary to build a monument gifted to the City of Providence in memory of his maternal grandfather, Governor Elisha Dyer.

The life-size bronze is a striking depiction of a young athlete falconing. This full-length partially nude male is typical of Victorian era garden statuary. The falcon is shown with wings spread wide, landing on the outstretched hand of the young man, while the figure's eyes and the falcon's eyes are fixed on each other. The statue, "full of dynamic tension and movement"[22] was originally located in the center of Pleasure Lake on a much more suitable fountain base on which were the heads of four rugged old men making even more prominent

---

[21] Daniel Wanton Lyman 1844-1886 An Appreciation
[22] Outdoor Sculpture of RI

the physical perfection of the athlete. The 1963 rehabilitation of the Japanese Garden caused its removal from the lake and relocation to the front of the birdhouse. The monument currently stands on a three-tiered granite base in the middle of a traffic island in the northeast area of Roger Williams Park.

The bronze is the 1889 creation of Henry Husdon Kitson, the famed sculptor who was commissioned for this work soon after he completed the bronze of Mayor Thomas Doyle.

GENERAL CASIMIR PULASKI EQUESTRIAN

Dedicated on "Justice for Poland Day" in 1953, this life-size bronze equestrian of Polish military hero General Casimir Pulaski commemorated the 200ᵗʰ anniversary of his birth. Pulaski fought to secure American liberty in the American Revolution and security for his native land of Poland. (Photo by Paul Caranci)

Casimir Pulaski was very possibly emulating his father's patriotism when, at an early age, he became involved in the political and revolutionary affairs of the Polish-Lithuanian Commonwealth. He is believed to have been born on March 6, 1745 in Warsaw, Poland and at a tender age of 17 began his military career soon becoming one of the leading military commanders for the Bar Confederation that fought against Russian domination of the Commonwealth in his native country. The uprisings failure, however, caused Pulaski into exile. Yet, the extraordinary bravery and leadership qualities of the Roman Catholic warrior were not lost on American patriot Benjamin Franklin who urged Pulaski to immigrate to North America and join the patriot cause in the American Revolution.

It didn't take long for Pulaski's spirit, determination and leadership to influence the favorable outcome of the war for American independence. Serving the cause as a Brigadier General, Pulaski's legion had written to General George Washington, "I came here, where freedom is being defended, to serve it, and to live or die for it." He met with an impressed Washington for the first time outside of Philadelphia on August 20, 1777 having arrived in America almost a month earlier.

His first military engagement was on September 11th at the Battle of Brandywine, even before he was given his appointment of service. As the line of the Continental Army troops began to yield, Pulaski met with Washington's contingent of about 30 men and reported that the British were cutting off the line of retreat. Following Washington's orders, Pulaski collected as many of the scattering troops as possible so as to secure a safe retreat. Pulaski, however, reorganized the troops and his subsequent charge averted a disastrous defeat, bringing him instant fame and saving the life of George Washington. As a result, Congress ordered Washington to assign Pulaski the rank of brigadier general in the Continental Army cavalry, a rank he proudly accepted on September 15, 1777.

Immediately, Pulaski reformed the fledgling cavalry that was scattered into four different regimens, and being used primarily for scouting services, by writing the first regulations for the formation. In his new role as Brigadier General he participated in the Battle of Germantown and spent the winter of 1777 and 1778 with the army at Valley Forge. His proposal that the military engagements continue throughout the harsh winter months was rejected by Washington, but provides an indication of Pulaski's dedication to the cause of American liberty. He used those months instead to reorganize the cavalry force primarily stationed in Trenton, NJ. While there, he joined with General Anthony Wayne in an attack on British Lt. Colonel Thomas Stearling's troops while they waited for better weather in order to cross the Delaware. During the ensuing engagement Pulaski's horse was shot out from under him but only a few of his men were wounded. Pulaski was later commended by General Wayne for his heroic actions in that engagement.

While Pulaski proved a valiant and brilliant leader, his leadership was not without difficulty. His leadership style introduced tactics and disciplinary measures radically different from those that the colonists were accustomed to and some of the officers serving under him resented taking orders from a foreigner who could barely speak English. Discontent over delays in pay was sometimes taken out on him and Pulaski's domineering personality was the source of frequent displeasure.

Considering the sentiment of his officers and troops Pulaski resigned his general command. Congress, however, at the recommendation of General Horatio Gates created a new unit of 68 lancers and 200 light infantry and gave Pulaski his previous rank over that unit adding a special title of "Commander of the Horse." The new force was headquartered in Baltimore and became known as the Pulaski Cavalry Legion. Though still demanding, he trained his men by using more traditional cavalry tactics. To further avoid feelings of resentment, Pulaski paid his men with his own money when the Patriot resources were low, therefore assuring that his forces would have the finest equipment with which to fight and protect themselves. Though questions of impropriety with the Legion's finances arose, and plagued him for the balance of his career, Pulaski was cleared of all charges after his death.

That death came all too soon! While serving on the southern front, Pulaski's forces tried to bolster a fledgling attack of British troops. Led by General Benjamin Lincoln, commander of the southern army, the joint forces, with French assistance, embarked on an attempt to retake Savannah. Soon after capturing a British outpost near Ogeechee River, the contingent encountered trouble. The French forces began to break and while Pulaski attempted to rally them he was mortally wounded by grapeshot, a mass of small metal balls or slugs packed tightly into a canvas bag and fired from cannon. Pulaski was carried from the field and brought aboard the *Wasp*, a privateer merchant ship. He never regained consciousness and died two days later. Marquis de Lafayette personally laid the cornerstone to a monument erected in Savannah, Georgia in his honor, further attesting to the high esteem in which he was held.

Pulaski has been honored for his contributions to the cause of American liberty on many occasions and in numerous ways. Congress authorized statues and monuments to his honor and designated October 11th of each year as General Pulaski Memorial Day with a large parade to be held in New York in celebration. In 1931 the General Casimir Pulaski United States 2 cent postage stamp was issued and on November 6, 2009, President Barack Obama signed a joint resolution of Congress conferring honorary citizenship upon Pulaski. Only 6 other people have been so honored.

Rhode Island's statue is a life-size bronze equestrian dedicated on "Justice for Poland Day" in 1953 marking the 200th anniversary of his birth. It depicts Pulaski raising a sword high in his right hand and riding a horse which is rearing up from an inclined plane and is the creation of local artist Guido Nincheri of Woonsocket whose paintings decorate the interiors of several Rhode Island churches. Among the more than 300 people who attended the dedication ceremony were US Senators Theodore Francis Green, John O. Pastore and Governor Dennis J. Roberts.

Speaking of Pulaski's efforts to secure American liberty as well as to the threat of Communist domination over Pulaski's homeland of Poland, Senator Pastore told the assembly, "No nation can remain free… if the rest of the world is covered in a blanket of Slavery."

THE PANCRATIAST
aka The Boxer

The Pancratiast portrays an athlete in the ancient Roman combat sport called Pankration, a sport incorporated into Greek Olympic Games in 648 BC. This is a 1900 replica of a statue found in a wall of the Temple of Sun during an excavation. (Photo by Heather Caranci

● ● ●

The ancient Romans incorporated the original sculpture of the Pancratiast in the Temple of the Sun where in 1885 it was discovered implanted in one of the Temple's walls during an excavation. In 1900 this replica was shipped to Paul Bajnotti in Providence and gifted to the City.

Pankration was a combat sport that was incorporated into the Greek Olympic Games in 648 BC. Founded as a mélange of boxing and wrestling, the game had scarcely any rules. The only things not acceptable were biting and gouging of the opponent's eyes. Though the Romans had little respect for the Greeks, a people they considered to be of a "slightly lower order of human being," they apparently liked the sport which was introduced in Rome by Caligula sometime between the years 37-41AD.[23]

In the bronze statue of this seated nude, the athlete looks strong, but exhausted as if recovering from a recent match. He is bearded and wears protective hand gear to his middle forearms. Appearing as if seated on a large rock, his head is turned to the right and he gazes upward in an unsettled pose.

---

[23] Hidden Treasures, p. 68.

BOWEN R. CHURCH

Aristede Berto Cianfarani sculpted this statue of Bowen R. Church, a talented cornet player who inspired thousands with his music. Though performing nationally and appearing at the Columbian World's Fair in Chicago in 1893, Church always enjoyed his frequent performances at the Roger Williams Park Bandstand located within earshot of his likeness. (Photo by Heather Caranci)

Nine year old Bowen Church boldly approached band director D. W. Reeves while the two were riding a train. Placing his clarinet to his lips Church played a melodic tune. The exercise resulted in the offer of free lessons and helped launch a career in which, at the age of only 18, Church became a featured soloist with the American Band of Providence. Church practiced incessantly and inspired others to take up the cornet. So impressed was Reeves with Church's talent that the two would frequently play duets with the band. They performed at the Columbian World's Fair in Chicago in 1893 and though receiving offers from other band leaders, Bowen never accepted them.

Reeves died in 1900 leaving Bowen to suffer from occasional bouts of drinking, a habit that began to negatively impact, and ultimately interrupt his heretofore brilliant career. Despite those issues Church was allowed to conduct the orchestra for a short time. Toward the end of his career Church moved to Jersey City where he later directed the orchestra of the Atlantic and Pacific Tea Company. No commercial recordings by Church are known to exist.

William G. James, gifted a statue of his friend Bowen to the City. It was sculpted by Aristide Berto Cianfarani and was dedicated on August 26, 1928. Bowen is depicted in a standing pose wearing a band uniform. His arms are raised and he is holding a cornet to his mouth. The life-size bronze likeness was cast by the Gorham Company and honors the career of the talented musician that so often entertained the public at Roger Williams Park. The City appropriately located the statue near Dalrymple Boathouse on an island behind the Park's casino across from the bandstand where Church so often appeared at outdoor concerts.

ABRAHAM LINCOLN

American historian and Lincoln expert to the Library of Congress Roy P. Basler believes that Rhode Island sculptor Gilbert Franklin captured the pose of this life-size bronze statue of Abraham Lincoln just after the President delivered the Gettysburg Address. (Photo by Heather Caranci)

In 1922 Henry W. Harvey, a prominent jewelry manufacturer, and his wife, bequeathed a sum of money to the City for a sculptor, to be chosen by the executor of the estate in conjunction with the Providence Art Club and the Rhode Island School of Design (RISD), to craft an undesignated statue in their memory. Local sculptor Gilbert Franklin, who also chaired the Fine Arts Division of RISD, created several models that he sent to New York for casting.

The funds finally became available in the early 1950s and the "committee" responded to calls from the time of Harvey's bequest to cast a statue of Abraham Lincoln. Franklin's life-size bronze of Lincoln was the group's choice. The statue is mounted on a ten ton granite base and depicts the President in classic pose with arms resting by his side and wearing traditional period cloths. In his right hand appears to be a piece of paper, perhaps his notes or speech from Gettysburg. According to Roy P. Basler, American historian and Lincoln expert to the Library of Congress, the sculptor caught the President just after giving the Gettysburg Address.

Basler spoke eloquently at the dedication ceremony. In his presentation he cited Lincoln's tolerance, perhaps "as a counterpoint to the spirit of McCarthyism" that pervaded that period of the 1950s[24].

---

[24] Hidden Treasures, p. 70.

COW ISLAND PROJECT

The Cow Island Project is actually a series of vertical and horizontal rectangles carefully placed on one of the Park's many islands. The strategic placement allows the viewer to move through them sequentially. Unfortunately the island is no longer accessible to the public without a boat. (Photo courtesy of the Rhode Island State Archives, Preston Collection, C#858)

It might appear as a series of concrete bases upon which nothing was ever mounted, but this series of vertical and horizontal rectangles are actually the completed work of Richard Fleischner.

In 1977, Fleischner carefully placed these granite platforms on one of the Park's many islands in such a way as to allow the viewer to move through them sequentially. However, the removal of the bridge to Cow Island, a key element to the original sculpture, makes that mission a virtual impossibility without benefit of a boat.

In addition to the bridge, the original sculpture contained a granite threshold, two parallel granite strips, two granite steps, two granite vertical markers with a granite rectangle embedded in the

• • •

earth. Unlike other sculptures in and around the park, the placement of this one on Cow Island seems immovable.

UNION SOLDIER
The Skirmisher

Dedicated in 1898, the Union Soldier was the first full-length bronze produced by the Gorham Company. It is a reproduction of a Kohlhagen statue originally cast for placement at Gettysburg in honor of the soldiers of the 39th Pennsylvania. (Photo by Heather Caranci)

• • •

He is wearing the military uniform of a Union infantry soldier and appears determined in his ascent up an imaginary hill. The soldier brandishes his bayoneted rifle in his right hand. Designed by Frederick Kohlhagen in 1895 and dedicated in 1898, this cast was the first full-length bronze produced by the Gorham Company. Kohlhagen designed the original for placement in Gettysburg. There it is known as The Skirmisher and is mounted on a bronze pedestal. The Gettysburg statue honors the soldiers of the 39th Pennsylvania. The Providence version, known simply as The Union Soldier, was gifted to the city by the Providence Association of Mechanics and Manufacturers and placed near the Temple to Music at its 1898 dedication. In 1993, however, it was relocated to the eastern entrance of the Park on the Miller Avenue traffic island and is mounted on a large boulder

• • •

DEMING MEMORIAL

This striking semi-circular bronze bench is the work of sculptor William Cowper and was produced in honor of the accomplishments of Roger Williams Park Commissioner Richard H. Deming who played an instrumental role in the development of the Park's physical landscape and programming. (Photo by Heather Caranci)

This beautiful semi-circular bronze bench was designed by W. C. Codman and sculpted by William Cowper in honor of the accomplishments of Richard H. Deming, the President of the Board of Park Commissioners from 1892 to 1902. During that time Deming played an instrumental role in the development of the park's physical landscape and programming.

The plinth that rises high from the center of the bench's backrest supports a bust-length portrait sculpture of Deming. The memorial bench, which is wrapped with vines, leaves and acorns in relief, was cast by the Gorham Company in 1904.

THE FIGHTING GLADIATOR

With arms raised high, The Fighting Gladiator appears as if he is engaged in the Roman games. This bronze reproduction of an iconic Roman marble was gifted to the Park by Gorham Company superintendent George Wilkinson. (Photo by Heather Caranci)

Like the Falconer and the Pancratiast before, the Fighting Gladiator depicts a male athlete in bronze. The figure is in motion as if in "the games." His arms are raised, one in front of him and one behind and his legs are outstretched in a running form.

This cast is modeled after a Roman marble that has been the object of admiration and study by artists and students alike for over 400 years. In fact, several copies have been made and can be found in many of the great houses throughout Europe.

This cast was done by the Gorham Company in 1891 and gifted to the Park by Gorham Superintendent George Wilkinson.

ROGER WILLIAMS MONUMENT

This 19ᵗʰ century postcard image depicts the Roger Williams Monument, one of the finest in the park bearing his name. This commemorative fulfills the terms of Betsy Williams' will requiring that a monument to the founder be placed on the land she donated to the City for use as a park. Betsy William's house can be seen to the left of the statue. (Post card image from the author's collection)

Fittingly, the statue of the City's founder is perhaps the most impressive of the Parks inventory. The 7 ½' tall standing bronze statue of Roger Williams is set upon the top of a 27' tall granite monument. At the base are 5 steps ascending to the shaft from every direction. A six feet high bronze female figure in classical draperies and sandals represents Clio, the Muse of history, and stands at the top step writing Williams' name on a bronze plaque that is set into the granite pedestal "figuratively entering his name into history."[25]

Williams is dressed in the seventeenth century cloths of a clergyman and has on a long coat. His hair is shoulder-length. In mid-

---

[25] Hidden Treasures, p.63.

stride, Williams carries a book with the inscribed words, "Soul" and "Liberty," in his left hand. His right arm is slightly outstretched.

The monument fulfills the terms of Betsy Williams' will which requires that a monument to the founder be erected in a park that will bear his name. A design competition resulted in the submission of 18 designs from which Franklin Simmons's plans were accepted by the Park Commissioners in 1874.

Simmons completed his original marble work in Munich. It was sent to Washington, D.C. where, in 1872, it was installed in the old U.S. House of Representatives following the expansion of the Capitol building. There it joins many other iconic American heroes in Statuary Hall. The statues on this monument were cast at Royal Foundry.

A parade from Market Square in downtown Providence to the Park preceded the dedication ceremony that was held on October 16, 1877 and attended by twenty thousand people. At the time of the dedication, the monument contained smaller ancillary pieces that included a shield, a scroll, a book and a pen all set at the muse's feet. These items were discovered missing at least as far back as the 1940s.

FERDINAND II

Ferdinand II was the repressive ruler of the Two Sicilies reigning for 29 years prior to Italy's unification. This statue was found buried in Naples in 1868 and purchased by Albert Dailey who donated it to Roger Williams Park after using it as a garden ornament for many years. (Photo by Paul Caranci

• • •
245

This repressive ruler served as the Sicilian Bourbon King of the Two Sicilies, a region formed by the union of the separate kingdoms of Sicily and Naples, forming Italy's largest region prior to the unification. He reigned for twenty-nine years beginning in 1830 and his violence didn't earn him many fans. After Garibaldi's victory in 1860 (see chapter 27), this statue and many other busts of the Bourbons were taken down and buried under its column. In 1868, the statue was rediscovered during an excavation and, while visiting Naples, Providence lumber merchant Albert Dailey acquired it for use as a garden ornament.

In 1881, Dailey donated the statue to the Park. The bust, located on Hilltop Avenue near Roosevelt Lake, is sculpted from white marble and depicts Ferdinand draped with a toga cloth. His face is turned slightly to the right. The bust is resting upon a tall granite plinth on a rectangular base.

MARCONI MEMORIAL

The Marconi Memorial was dedicated in 1953 to honor the Italian inventor, Guglielmo Marconi for his many accomplishments, including his pioneering work on long-distance radio transmissions. His efforts led to the development of the first effective system of radio communication. (Photo by Heather Caranci)

Shortly after the death of Guglielmo Marconi, the Italian-American community in Providence began a sixteen year effort to build a proper memorial to the Italian inventor. Their efforts bore fruit in 1953 with the October dedication of a monument in Roger Williams Park.

Marconi was born in Bologna, Italy, in 1874. He was a Nobel Prize-winning physicist and an inventor credited with pioneering work on long-distance radio transmissions. His experiments in wireless telegraphy led to the development of the first effective system of radio communication. It was therefore important to the City's Italian-American population that his contributions to the world be remembered through a memorial.

Designed by Oresto DiSaia and inscribed, "To Guglielmo Marconi, father of Wireless Telegraphy," the monument is an18'high granite described by Freeman and Lasky in *Hidden Treasures* as an "articulated shaft adorned with a frieze depicting wireless communications between different locations and means of transportation."[26]

The dedication ceremony was made more special by the attendance of Marconi's daughter. US Senator John O. Pastore and Governor Dennis J. Roberts also attended and spoke not only of Marconi's accomplishments but of those of the local Italian-American community as well.

---

[26] Hidden Treasures, p.69.

LIONS MEMORIAL

The Lions Memorial, dedicated on September 11, 1960, commemorates the contributions of the deceased members of the Lions Clubs of Rhode Island. The artist of the memorial is unknown. (Photo by Heather Caranci)

Prowling inside the confines of a low iron fence in the facility's west end is one of several lions living at Roger Williams Park. Rather than being contained in the zoo however, this feline, though barely restricted, poses no threat to visitors. The stone lion was a gift of the Lions Club International and was dedicated on September 11, 1960. Located near Pine Hill and Maple Avenue in the Park's west end, this stalking male lion rests atop a rectangular base that also displays the seal of the Lions Club International. The artist is unknown.

THE STONE EAGLE

Gail Whitsitt-Lynch designed The Stone Eagle and gifted it to Roger Williams Park which dedicated it in 1976. The eagle is made of concrete and was constructed over a wire frame. (Photo by Heather Caranci)

The painted concrete statue was designed by Gail Whitsitt-Lynch and is constructed over a wire frame. Located near Montgomery Street in the Park's west end, the statue depicts an eagle in a landing position. Its talons are outstretched and its wings are fully extended with the left wing slightly higher than the right. Whitsitt-Lynch is primarily a wood and stone carver, assemblage sculptor, and printmaker. Her work appears in numerous public and private collections, including this ferro-cement eagle that was dedicated in Roger Williams Park in 1976.

• • •

SRI CHINMOY –DREAMER OF PEACE
1931-2007

Chinmoy Kumar Ghose dedicated his life to the service of humanity. This renaissance man promoted peace through meditation, but was also a gifted artist, composer and poet. The Sri Chinmoy Oneness-Home Peace Run, founded in 1977, is still run by thousands today. (Photo by Heather Caranci)

Nothing in his early life in India might have provided a clue that Chinmoy Kumar Ghose, born the youngest of seven children on August 27, 1931, would one day influence the world through meditation. After moving to New York in 1964, however, Ghose, who is better known as Sri Chinmoy, established the first meditation center in Queens and over time would train thousands in the art of meditation in 60 countries of the world.

In April 1970, Chinmoy began leading "Peace Meditations at the United Nations" attended by employees and diplomats of the UN for over 37 years. He advocated respect for other religions and interfaith harmony noting the "oneness" of all religions.

Far more than someone who simply promoted peace through meditation, Chinmoy was a renaissance man of sorts. During a visit to Ottowa, Canada he decided to try his hand at painting. His works of abstract art have since been displayed in such impressive venues as the Louvre in Paris and in London's Victoria and Albert Museum. He composed thousands of musical compositions and gave hundreds of free peace concerts. He claimed to have written over 120,000 poems and recited poetry at the United Nations in 2001. His poetry was even read by NY Governor David Patterson at a ceremony marking the ninth anniversary of the terrorist attacks of 9/11.

Events he started include the Sri Chinmoy Marathon Team (founded in 1977 but expanded ten years later to become the Sri Chinmoy Oneness-Home Peace Run) that encourages fitness and conducts running, cycling, swimming and other athletic events worldwide, and the Sri Chinmoy strength exhibitions established to promote weight lifting, something Chinmoy began doing in 1985 at the age of 54.

After dedicating his life to the service of humanity, Chinmoy died at the age of 76 on October 11, 2007. On April 18, 2011 a bronze statue was dedicated near the Botanical Center of Roger Williams Park in memory of this "Dreamer of Peace." The statue depicts Chinmoy in traditional Indian dress. Both arms are stretched out before him and his two hands clutch the peace torch, a symbol of humanity's eternal aspirations for inner and outer peace. Years earlier, on July 27, 1982, a "peace tree" was planted in the Park marked with a concrete stone inscribed, "May my aspiring and loving heart's gratitude-plant grow upward every day." - Sri Chinmoy.

ROTARY CLUB FOUNTAIN OF 1926

The beautiful Rotary Club Fountain of 1926, though restored by the Providence Rotary Club in conjunction with the Providence Parks Department in 2010, has once again fallen into a state of disrepair, probably the result of vandalism. (Photo by Heather Caranci)

● ● ●

255

Originally located behind Roger Williams Park's Museum of Natural History, this beautiful fountain with mosaic tiles was relocated to the Botanical Center just in time for the Club's centennial celebration. Gifted to the City by the Rotary Club of Providence in 1926, the fountain is the work of John Cuddy. It was restored by the Providence Rotary Club in conjunction with officials of the Providence Parks Department in 2010.

• • •

HAITIAN MEMORIAL

The Haitian Memorial is the first monument in Roger Williams Park dedicated to the memory of the Haitian Freedom Fighters who fought for the liberation of Saint Domingue from its colonial bonds between 1791 and 1804. (Photo by Heather Caranci)

The 2005 creation of a memorial plaza in Roger Williams Park marked the first time that a memorial was dedicated in the memory of the Haitian Freedom Fighters. Though this particular memorial specifically honors Toussaint Louverture and Jean-Jacques Dessalines, two Haitian Freedom Fighters who fought for the liberation of Saint Domingue from its colonial bonds between 1791 and 1804, it generally honors all Haitians who sacrificed for the cause of freedom.

As noted on the memorial plaque mounted in the granite stone, Louverture and Dassalines were "armed with the conviction that slavery and servitude had no justifiable place within human society in a civilized world, and under the banner of the Declaration of the Rights of Man, their devotion to democratic principles was realized in the creation of the Republic of Haiti after 13 years of constant struggle."

The creation of the memorial park was a project of the Lakay Foundation, Inc. in recognition of the critical leadership of Louverture and Dessalines to the cause of Haitian freedom. The August 14, 2005 dedication ceremony was in remembrance of the Bicentennial of Haitian Independence.

DAVID WALLIS REEVES FOUNTAIN 1838-1900

Commemorating the life of one of the truly accomplished cornetist, the David Wallis Reeves Fountain honors the man who conducted the American Band of Providence, wrote operettas, polkas quadrilles, idylls, reveries and over 100 marches. (Photo by Heather Caranci)

David Wallis Reeves was only fourteen in 1852 when he began playing in the Oswego Band. He later left home to follow the Dan Rice Circus band just to study under Eb cornetist Thomas Canham. In 1860 he began touring with Rumsey & Newcombe Minstrels and only two-years later played solo coronet with the Dodworth Band at the Lucy Rushton Theater in New York.

In 1866 he began conducting the American Band of Providence where he wrote operettas, polkas quadrilles, idylls, reveries and over 100 marches, making the group one of the most prestigious performing organizations in the United States. He believed that the quality of music was not in its melodic content, but rather in how the music was played, and he was a pioneer in using countermelodies in his own marches.

• • •

Reeves was asked to conduct the Gilmore Band at the 1893 Columbian Exposition in Chicago and the 1894 Pittsburg Exposition. A successful band leader, performer and teacher (he taught Bowen Church and many others), Reeves died on March 8, 1900.

In 1926 a fountain was dedicated in his honor at Roger Williams Park. Eleven thousand people attended the dedication, as testament to Reeves' "rock star" status at the time. Located near the carousel, the monument is a simple water fountain, built with marble and designed by William T. Aldrich in the classic Greek style. The shaft is ornamented with intertwining fruits, flowers and lyres. The top is designed as a concave so as to enable it to serve as a birdbath as well.

JUAN PABLO DUARTE

He sacrificed his own wealth to finance and supervise the Dominican War of Independence. In 2003, the Latino community honored Juan Pablo Duarte's sacrifice with the first monument placed in Roger Williams Park in honor of a Hispanic/Latino. (Photo by Heather Caranci)

Born on January 26, 1813, Juan Pablo Duarte was one of the founding fathers of the Dominican Republic. He helped create La Trinitaria, a political and military organization used to fight against Haitian occupation, achieve independence, and create a self-sufficient nation established on liberal ideals of a democratic government.

Duarte sacrificed his own wealth to finance and supervise the Dominican War of Independence, something that led to his financial ruin. At the time, some of his views were considered so radical, even by his own people, that he was periodically exiled following the founding of the new nation. This notion does not seem possible in light of the fact that his democratic ideals have served as a guiding principle for most modern Dominican governments.

• • •

Juan Pablo eventually died in exile from the very nation he helped create making him a true martyr in the eyes of subsequent generations. In 2002-03 the Latino community honored Juan Pablo Duarte's memory and sacrifice with the establishment of a Juan Pablo Duarte Square. The monument placed in his honor is the first Hispanic/Latino monument to be erected in Roger Williams Park.

Chapter 24

Prospect Terrace

184 Pratt Street at Congdon Street

ROGER WILLIAMS MEMORIAL

After his remains were located and relocated 3 times, the Roger Williams Memorial in Prospect Park is the final resting place of the State's founder. The Westerly granite statue, dedicated on June 29, 1939, stands at 14.5'tall and provides a spectacular view of the city Williams founded. (Postcard image from the author's collection)

In 1890, ten years after the Providence Association of Mechanics and Manufacturers conceived of a monument to Roger Williams, Stephen Randall, a direct descendent of Williams, organized a Memorial Association with the blessing of the state legislature. Randall was concerned that Williams grave site, then in the yard of the 109 Benefit Street home owned by Sullivan Dorr but on land once owned by Roger Williams, was wholly unbefitting a man of Williams' importance. It was left unmarked and the exact location was all but forgotten. Though developing very specific plans for a suitable monument, the project did not reach fruition.

Some 44 years later, however, in anticipation of the tercentenary of Roger Williams' founding of Providence, the general assembly incorporated a new Memorial Association with a goal of erecting a monument to Williams on Prospect Terrace of sufficient height to be viewed from a significant distance, two conditions of Randall's

• • •

will and bequest. The designs of Ralph T. Walker and Leo Freidlander emerged victorious from a competition conducted by the Association. Their plans included a stairway that would connect the terrace with the park below. In the park, a central pool would be flanked by two Indians. This design was later abandoned, however, in favor of the current monument.

On June 29, 1939 a Westerly granite statue of Williams was dedicated. It stands about 14 1/2 feet tall between two granite pylons that form a rectangular arch projecting slightly from the terrace. The figure of Williams is shown to be blessing the city as he stands at the bow of his canoe. After following a circuitous route that took the founder's remains from the Benefit Street yard to the North Burial Ground grave of Stephen Randall to a separate place of internment at the North Burial Ground, they were finally placed in a tomb beneath the eastern base of the monument where they lie today. This monument was placed on the National Register of Historic Places as part of the College Hill Historic District. Prospect Terrace Park is located on Congden Street on the City's East Side and offers spectacular views of the City.

Chapter 25

Roger Williams National Park

284 North Main Street

HAHN MEMORIAL

The Roger Williams National Park is the location of the Hahn Memorial, a monument surrounding the natural spring used by Roger Williams in rendering that spot the perfect place to make settlement in 1636. The lot on which Williams built his first house is located across the street and marked with a bronze plaque on the 2ⁿᵈ floor of the building. (Photo by Paul Caranci)

Shortly after landing on the shores of Providence in 1636, Roger Williams continued his westward trek to the shores of the Providence River. There he discovered a natural spring rendering this spot on modern day North Main Street the perfect place to make settlement. In thanksgiving to God, Williams named the area Providence. Williams built a small house on a lot on the easterly side of North Main Street, almost directly across from the spring. Later development banished all evidence of the spring to the basement of a building, but in 1930, Superior Court Judge J. Jerome Hahn purchased the building and had it demolished. He then donated the land to the City in memory of his father who is remembered as the City's first publicly elected person of Jewish faith.

● ● ●

The memorial consists of a large wall with a center stairway that leads from either side to the sidewalk above. It is the design of Norman Isham and was dedicated in 1933. The Colonial style wall and stairway is surrounded by a peaceful garden whose focal point is a well curb that encircles the original spring.

Chapter 26

Burnside Park

2 Kennedy Plaza

MAJOR GENERAL AMBROSE BURNSIDE EQUESTRIAN

The Major General Ambrose Burnside Equestrian statue commemorates the Civil War General and Governor of Rhode Island. Though a beautiful statue, the general was rated one of the top ten worse by Civil War historians. The statue has been the object of vandalism and protests have been held at its base. (Photo by Heather Caranci)

Visitors will easily locate this 13 ½ foot equestrian bronze statue tucked in the northeast corner of this downtown park dedicated to the life and career of Civil War Major General Ambrose Burnside. The statue was suggested by Civil War hero Colonel Isaac M. Potter on the day following Burnside's untimely death in 1881 and was commissioned by Launt Thompson, a renowned 19th century sculptor from New York responsible for many of the soldiers and sailors monuments completed after the Civil War. The Burnside statue was the final work of the brilliant career of the man once described as most gifted monument builder in America.

When first dedicated in 1887, the statue was located on the exact spot now occupied by the Federal Building. Standing on a 28' high granite base designed by New York artist Henry O. Avery, the statue faced the Soldiers and Sailors monument that was originally situated at the opposite end of Exchange Place (now Kennedy Plaza) in front of City Hall. In 1906, however, during a major reconfiguration of the area following the construction of Union Station, the statue was moved to its present location. The design of the base was modified at that time by General William R. Walker, a prominent architect from Providence.

General Burnside graduated from West Point in 1847. He served in the Mexican War and was assigned to Fort Adams in Newport where he met and later married Mary Bishop of Providence. In 1853, Burnside resigned his commission in pursuit of a business career manufacturing rifles in Bristol. During that time he invented the Burnside breech-loading rifle. Neither the gun nor the business was successful however and Burnside accepted a position with Illinois Central Railroad, in the mid-west, a bit closer to his birthplace of Liberty, Indiana. With the start of the Civil War Burnside left that job and answered the call of Rhode Island Governor William Sprague to command the First Rhode Island Volunteers.

Just about 1 ½ years into the war, Burnside, who was highly regarded by President Abraham Lincoln, reluctantly accepted the President's appointment to command of the Army of the Potomac replacing General George McClellan who Lincoln believed was not aggressive enough in his pursuit of the Confederate Army. Burnside immediately provided a spark to the North with early victories in North Carolina achieving some of the few Union triumphs in the early stages of the Civil War. However, his star soon faded as he was handed responsibility for embarrassing defeats at Fredericksburg and Petersburg. It was the 4-day battle of Fredericksburg in December 1862 however, that most damaged his career. The defeat was one of the most lopsided of all the battles of the Civil War. Thirteen thousand Union soldiers were killed, wounded or missing. Confederate casualties by contrast numbered only about 4,000. Burnside accepted full responsibility saying, "For the failure in the attack I am responsible as the extreme gallantry, courage and endurance shown by them [the troops] was never excelled. To the families and friends of the dead I

• • •

can only offer my heartfelt sympathy." The apology did little to quell the horror of Northern families, however, and Burnside's reputation as a General never truly recovered from these losses. Lincoln removed Burnside from command of the Army of the Potomac two months later. Despite some subsequent bright spots in his military career, Burnside resigned his commission on April 15, 1865 following a second major gaff during the siege of Petersburg that resulted in a great number of Union casualties.

After the war, Burnside returned to his native Rhode Island where he was three times elected to one-year terms as governor in 1866, 1867 and 1868. In 1875 and again in 1881 he was elected by the RI State Senate to a seat in the United States Senate, but on September 13, 1881, at the age of 57, he died suddenly of neuralgia of the heart (Angina Pectoris) at his Bristol home, shortly after the start of his second term.

Of his three careers, business, military and politics, the latter was certainly the most successful. According to William Thayer Burnside was a true patriot who "by personal magnetism held a sure lodgment in the hearts of most of those who knew him. His jovial, cheerful temperament carried sunshine into all circles. Trustful himself, he suspected no guile in others; hence was ill fitted to contend against the wiles of the world, by which he was often circumvented and his business projects brought to naught. But in official station his personal popularity and the confidence reposed in his integrity brought to him no small measure of success." As an elected official he was "industrious, incorruptible, and intelligent in the discharge of the various duties entrusted to him."

The statue was paid with $40,000 raised by public subscription ranging from 25 cents to $1,000. In addition, $10,000 in state assistance approved by the General Assembly and $5,000 from the City of Providence assisted the effort. Thousands of residents and dignitaries, including General William T. Sherman, attended the dedication whose principal address was delivered by RI General and RI Historical Society President Horatio Rogers, who served under Sherman's command. During his remarks, Rogers said, "His career is ended, his statue is done. Ambrose E. Burnside has passed into history. Rhode Island has spared naught that could attest her appreciation. In life she conferred her highest honors and dignities upon him; in death she has

• • •

fashioned his form and feature in bronze, graven his name in granite, and reared them aloft in enduring testimony of her gratitude, and as an example for emulation."[27]

Over the years both Burnside's statue and his reputation have suffered. The statue of the man recently listed among the top ten worse generals of the war by Civil War historians was desecrated during the 1969 annual arts festival with multi-colored paints creating a psychedelic effect. Sandblasting was required to remove the graffiti from the statue and base. In 2013, the Occupy Providence movement set up a "tent city" in Burnside Park holding assemblies at the statue's base. Protesters covered the statue with signs and banners, tied a mask over Burnside's face and affixed a flag to the horse's tail. The protestors were allowed to "occupy" the area for several weeks before reaching an accord with Mayor Angel Tavares ending the occupation.

---

[27]Dedication of the Equestrian Statue of Major General Ambrose E. Burnside, July 4, 1887, With the Oration of General Horatio Rogers, E.L. Freeman & Sons, Printers & Publishers, 1887

BAJNOTTI FOUNTAIN
Carrie Brown Memorial

Perhaps the most beautiful of all of the fountains in Providence is the Bajnotti Fountain in Burnside Park. Gifted to the City in 1901 by the broken-hearted husband of Carrie Brown Bajnotti, the fountain is an enduring symbol of an extraordinary love story. (Postcard image from the author's collection)

By the time that Caroline "Carrie" Mathilde Brown was born October 28, 1841, her sister Annmary Brown (3/9/1837) was already four and a half years old, but the two were interminably close. The granddaughters of Nicholas Brown Jr., the benefactor for whom Brown University is named, had a third sister who died just days after Annmary's birth. Nicholas III and Carline Mathilde Clements Brown, the grief stricken parents, gave Annmary their deceased daughter's name.

In 1846, while living in New York, Nicholas III received an appointment by President Polk as US Consul-General in Rome and the family moved abroad. The girls first received their education in convents in Rome and Geneva but, since his appointment had expired in 1849, the family moved back to Providence, Rhode Island after Annmary's graduation from Madame Arlaud's School in Geneva in 1854.

• • •

In Rhode Island, the family spent their summers at Choppe-quonsett, their 2nd home located on Narragansett Bay. It was here in 1860 that Annmary married future Civil War troop leader Rush Hawkins of New York City. Annmary, who long suffered from severe respiratory ailments, seemed the worse during the four years that her husband was away at war. During that time Carrie acted as both her companion and caretaker drawing an even closer bond between them. At War's end, Rush and Annmary spent a great deal of time traveling leaving Carrie, now in her thirties, feeling the eternal spinster.

Fortunes changed, however, when Italian Count and Diplomat Paul Bajnotti arrived in Rhode Island in 1875. The two fell quickly in love and were soon married in an impressive ceremony also held at the summer home. Over the course of their lives the couple would live wherever Paul's European diplomatic postings took them. With the Hawkins' searching the globe for a cure for Annmary's lung affliction, the sisters were reunited for great lengths in Europe. The brothers-in-law also became close in their shared adoration of their wives and the four acted as best friends.

Surprisingly, it was Carrie, and not Annmary who succumbed to lung disease when her bout with the flu developed into pneumonia in Palermo, Italy. She died in 1893 leaving Paul "sorrowing and heartbroken," Hawkins would later write. She was buried in an English cemetery in Rome. Paul was determined, however, to immortalize Carrie in her hometown of Providence which he would do with two monuments. The first, commissioned five years after her death, is the Carrie Brown Bajnotti Memorial Fountain located in Burnside Park.

Unveiled on June 26, 1901, this "gift" to the City is located at the approach to Union Station. It was cast by the Gorham Company and is comprised of four bronze statues at the center of a granite basin that contains 234 spray outlets and a pinnacle spout. The four bronze figures represent the "Struggle of Life." Life, symbolized by an angel wearing a mantle of truth that seems to be flowing from its shoulders, is struggling to break free from "duty, passion and avarice," represented by three bronze male figures. Despite the attempts to keep its soul, the angel and life are held down by the earthly tendencies.

Inscribed in the granite are the words, "ERECTED AD MDCCCC A GIFT TO HONOR THE MEMORY OF CARRIE MATHILDE DAUGHTER OF THE LATE NICHOLAS BROWN

OF PROVIDENCE FROM HER HUSBAND PAUL BAJNOTTI OF TURIN ITALY."

This dramatic depiction is the work of sculptor Enid Yandell who studied under Rodin. Over the course of the 20th century, the monument fell into various stages of disrepair. It was restored in 2002 by the Providence architectural firm of Durkee, Brown, Viveiros and Werenfels.

Ten years after the death of Carrie, Annmary also developed pneumonia reuniting with her sister in death after a brief illness in 1903. Hawkins wrote, "No words at my command are equal to the expression of my desolation and loneliness. The present is without joy and the future a dreary anticipation. Hawkins was very probably inspired by his brother-in-law to have a mausoleum and museum built to her memory at 21 Brown Street in Providence. Completed in 1907, the memorial served not only as a final resting place for the couple, but also a museum for his extensive book collection, paintings and Civil War relics and other personal collections. The enscription on the marble floor slab that marks his wife's burial site reads, "Like some rare flower entombed in its beauty, shedding everlasting."

Bajnotti died in 1919 in Turin, Italy. Hawkins passed away a year later when struck by a car in New York City. Every year until his last, Hawkins left fresh flowers at the tomb of Annmary on her birthday and provided sufficient funds in his will to continue that tradition, which carries on to this very day.

Paul's second monument to Carrie was a clock tower built on the campus of Brown University. Its description can be found in Chapter 1.

THE SCOUT

Lt. Colonel Henry Harrison is the subject of The Scout. The 1911 life-size bronze remembers the service of General Philip Sheridan's Civil War brigade of courageous "scouts" to provide intelligence reports during the war.(Photo by Heather Caranci)

● ● ●

Civil War Lieutenant Colonel Henry Harrison, one of the most famous spies of the Civil War, is the subject of this 1911 bronze statue. Standing opposite General Ambrose Burnside in the park that bears his name stands this life-size soldier dressed in period military uniform wearing tall boots and a brimmed hat. An additional small gun is tucked in his left boot.

The Scouts were a unit dispatched by General Philip Sheridan to provide intelligence reports to him during the Civil War. In statue, Young appears in mid-stride with a revolver hanging from his right hand.

Rhode Island School of Design teacher Henry Schonhardt, who also worked at the Gorham Manufacturing Co., and is perhaps better known for his State House statue of Nathanael Greene, sculpted The Scout which was cast by the Gorham Manufacturing Company. The statue is set upon a boulder on which is a tablet inscribed with the words of gratitude that Sheridan made in his report to the Secretary of War. According to comments made by Schonhardt at the dedication ceremony, he portrayed Young just as he caught the fearless guerrilla leader of the South. Governor Aram J. Pothier expressed his thanks for the historical accuracy of the bronze portrait saying that he hoped not only to immortalize Young, but to teach "the coming generations those lessons of loyalty, courage and integrity that are the most loveable attributes of manhood."

The keynote address was given by General Elisha H. Rhodes of the Second Rhode Island Regiment. Rhodes was one of only four surviving members of Sheridan's Scouts to attend the dedication ceremonies.

Chapter 27

Garibaldi Park

99 Atwells Avenue

GIUSEPPE GARIBALDI BUST

The 50ᵗʰ anniversary of the Italian Patriot's death provided the impetus to honor Giuseppe Garibaldi in bronze. Created by visiting Italian sculptor Filippo T. Sgarlatto the siting of the statue became quite controversial until the City's first Italo-American Mayor, Vincent Buddy Cianci, relocated the bust to its current Federal Hill location. (Photo by Heather Caranci)

On the fiftieth anniversary of the Italian Patriot's death, a group of sixty-two fraternal and patriotic organizations commissioned a bust of Giuseppe Garibaldi. The bronze bust was designed by Filippo T. Sgarlatto, an Italian sculptor that was visiting Providence and was cast by Cellini Bronze Works. Garibaldi is depicted wearing a cap and sporting a beard and a cape. The intent was to locate the figure at the rear of Union Station. However, when the bust was completed, Providence's Board of Parks Commissioners refused to accept it. The City Council was outraged and insulted and immediately rebuked the Commissioners. Mayor James Dunne said nothing in reply and the

● ● ●

council sought the assistance of Governor Norman Case. Case arranged for the installation of the bust at the Rhode Island College of Education (RICE).

On July 3, 1932, the bust was finally dedicated with various speakers comparing Garibaldi's beliefs with American virtues. They noted that both Garibaldi and George Washington "engaged in similar kinds of warfare, endured similar hardships, and culminated their careers as leaders of the governments. The principal speaker cited Garibaldi's ideals as the inspiration to help America out of its Depression difficulties, urging Italian-Americans to 'remember our great hero and devote our energy to the amelioration of the social order, to the betterment of man and to the propagation of those noble sentiments without which there would not have been a united Italy."[28] On October 13, 1975, Mayor Vincent "Buddy" Cianci, the City's first leader of Italian American decent, relocated the bust to a new park established on Federal Hill and dedicated to Garibaldi's honor. It rests on a new tall pedestal of engraved granite.

What was it about Garibaldi that prompted so much controversy in the first place?

Garibaldi was born in Nice, Italy on July 4, 1807 and christened Joseph Marie Garibaldi. Because of his family's involvement in the coastal trade, Garibaldi was drawn to the sea and was certified a merchant marine captain in 1832. On a trip to Russia in April 1833, Garibaldi met Giovanni Battista Cuneo, a politically active immigrant and protégé of Giuseppe Mazzini, an impassioned proponent of Italian unification as a liberal republic through political and social reform. Garibaldi joined La Giovine Italia / Young Italy, Mazzini's secret society, and pledge his oath to the struggle to liberate and unify Italy from Austrian dominance.

Following a meeting with Mazzini, Garibaldi joined the Carbonari revolutionary association and in February 1834 participated in an insurrection in Piedmont. In absentia a Genoese court sentenced Garibaldi to death and he fled to Marseille. He spent the next several years in Brazil and Uruguay, returning to Italy at the outbreak of the

---

[28]Hidden Treasure: Public Sculpture in Providence, Rhode Island Publication Society, for the RI Bicentennial Foundation, 1980.)

revolution in Palermo in January 1848 where he offered his services to a distrustful Charles Albert of Sardinia. Garibaldi moved on offering assistance instead to the provisional government of Milan which had rebelled against Austrian occupation. He later fought in the defense of Rome and led his army to an unlikely defeat of the far superior French army on April 30, 1849. He couldn't hold a fortified French response back, however and on June 30th he was able to convince the Roman Assembly, who had been discussing surrender, to retreat Rome and continue resistance from the Apennine Mountains.

Garibaldi orchestrated the "retreat" but his movement failed, causing him to sail to the United States in the hopes of acquiring a merchant ship with which to start a new business. Upon arriving in New York on July 30, 1850, however, he found that the planned financing for the vessel fell through. He took employment with Antonio Meucci in his Staten Island candle factory. Feeling unfulfilled, Garibaldi and a friend soon departed New York arriving first in Nicaragua then ultimately in Peru in late 1851. He accepted work as a ship captain hauling copper and wool and in 1852 he sailed for China. His travels took him back to the United States leaving this country for the last time in November 1853.

In May 1854 his exile from Italy ended and he returned to his homeland to offer his services in the Second Italian War of Independence. With a band of volunteers he secured victories over the Austrians at Varese, Como and other places but still longed for the French to return his birthplace of Nice to Italy. He spoke against Cavour for ceding Nice to the French Emperor Louis Napoleon and engaged in riots with like-minded nationalists.

Garibaldi recognized an opportunity to take more aggressive action in support of his cause when he learned of the April 1860 uprisings in Messina and Palermo. Gathering 800 volunteers he sailed to Marsala on May 11th and led his unlikely band of heroes to a victory over an enemy force of 1,500 men by employing a counter-intuitive tactic of an uphill bayonet charge. It was on this charge that he uttered in Italian his now famous words, "Here we either make Italy, or we die." The next day he declared himself dictator of Sicily in the name of Victor Emmanuel II of Italy and on May 27th he advanced to the Island capitol of Palermo where he launched a siege. Despite early advances, enemy reinforcements arrived and bombarded the capitol city to near ruin. Garibaldi's efforts gained him worldwide notoriety and the adulation of the Italian people. His reputation caused even Napoleon to question French success and by July, only the citadel resisted. By September Garibaldi's rank had swelled to 24,000, almost a man-for-man match of the Neapolitan army of 25,000 men, yet he couldn't secure final victory over Napoleon without the help of the Piedmontese who dictated stringent terms in exchange for their support. Garibaldi was forced to hand over all of his southern territorial gains and ultimately retired to the rocky island of Caprera.

He volunteered his services to Abraham Lincoln at the outbreak of the American Civil War and was offered a Major General's commission in the US Army, but, according to Italian historian Arrigo Petacco, Garibaldi's insistence that Lincoln state his expressed purpose of the war as the emancipation of the slaves was something Lincoln, at that time, was unwilling to do for fear that it would worsen an agricultural crisis.

In August 1862 Garibaldi took up arms again in an effort to gain Rome for Italy. The Pope of Rome enjoyed sovereign status and the protection of the French to ensure its continuance. Garibaldi's effort failed and he was wounded in a short battle. He was imprisoned for a short time near La Spezia, nursed back to health and released.

In 1866 Garibaldi made one final attempt to unite Italy, this time with the consent of the government and 40,000 troops. Joining Prussia against Austria-Hunary, he hoped to take Venetia from Austrian rule in what is considered Italy's Third War of Independence. While he did secure an Italian victory at Bezzecca, the only one of the war, it was Prussia's victory that secured the armistice by which Austria ceded Venetia to Italy.

In 1867 he made one final attempt to capture Rome from the Papal Army, but was wounded in the leg during the Battle of Mentana and forced to withdraw. He was again imprisoned by the Italian government but released after a time returning to the island of Caprera.

Even after defeat, imprisonment and self-imposed exile, he continued his efforts to free Rome for Italy proposing to abolish the papacy as the most harmful of all secret societies. By 1870, following the Franco-Prussian War, the attitudes of many Italians changed and the Italian Army accomplished what Garibaldi spent a lifetime trying to achieve; the capture of the Papal States from the Pope and the

• • •

French. By this time, however, Garibaldi had switched his allegiance to France where he assumed command of the volunteer Army of the Vosges. Even this didn't cause the Italian people to "venerate" him less. He was again elected to the Italian Parliament supporting an ambitious project of land reclamation in southern Lazio.

Garibaldi fought for many causes which today are protected in the United States. The League of Democracy, which he founded in 1879 advocated for universal suffrage, the emancipation of women and the maintenance of a standing army.

Garibaldi died on June 2, 1882 at the age of 75 and controversy followed him even unto death. Though his will provided for cremation his body was buried on Caprera alongside his wife and children. In 2012 his remains were exhumed to allow his descendants to confirm that the remains were in fact those of Garibaldi. It is uncertain what will happen to the remains if it is determined that they are his.

Garibaldi has gotten tributes all around the world. Five ships were named in his honor in Italy as was a school in Mansfield, Nottinghamshire. Statues stand in many Italian squares. His bust can be seen outside the entrance of the Supreme Court Chamber of the US Capitol in Washington, DC. In addition to Italy and the United States, there are statues of Garibaldi in Argentina, Brazil, Bulgaria, Buenos Aires, France, Hungary, Russia, Turkey, and Uraguay. Portraits can be found in even more nations.

So considering Garibaldi's international fame, patriotism and emphatic denunciation of slavery, why did Providence try to prevent the placement of his bust in the City? While we may never have a definitive answer to that question, Rhode Island Historian Laureate Dr. Patrick Conley notes that all four great architects of Italian independence, Mazzini, Cavour, Victor Emmanuel, and Garabaldi, ran afoul of the papacy. It is possible that the resistance to the Garibaldi bust stemmed from the Irish who ran Providence. They were ultramontane, or defenders of papal supremacy, and may have been offended at Garibaldi's history of attacks on the Pope. The fact that the papal nuncios were very influential with the Bishops of the Diocese of Providence may have been responsible for the Garibaldi dilemma.

Chapter 28

Blackstone Park

Blackstone Boulevard

THE SPIRIT OF YOUTH
aka A Memorial to Young Womanhood

The moving story of 15-year old Constance Witherby is memorialized with a 1933 bronze statue called The Spirit of Youth and located along the walking path between the travel lanes of Blackstone Blvd. Her poetry was posthumously published by her mother Dorothy in 1930. (Photo by Paul Caranci)

Each day hundreds of walkers, runners and bikers pass by a charming bronze figure of a woman located in a long narrow park between the two travel lanes of Blackstone Boulevard. Some stop to take a snapshot, some for a moment of silence, still others leave flowers as if it were a roadside memorial. Despite the different reactions, few fail to notice the figure of a beautiful woman with flowing hair blowing back in the imaginary breeze. She is impeccably dressed in a full-length, flowing sleeveless dress. She appears in motion, as if stepping off the rectangular piece of bronze that rests on a polished granite base about 3 feet high.

Though many pass by, few know the story of Constance Witherby, a student at Providence's Lincoln School who spent much of her time writing poetry, playing sports and engaging in activities that most adolescents would just dream about.

Four years after her graduation from Wellesley College in 1908, Dorothy Hazard, married Edwin C. Witherby. The couple had three children - Constance, born on September 5, 1913, Thomas born in 1915 and Frederick R.H. "Erik" born in 1917. Four years after the death of Edwin in 1919, Dorothy married Stephen Foster Hunt, an executive with Rhode Island's Nicholson File Company and the family set up residences in Providence and Narragansett. Together they had one more child, Deborah (Hunt) Philbrick in 1925.

Dorothy enjoyed the life of a Providence socialite. She was deeply involved in a wide variety of causes and was one of the early leaders of the Urban League in Rhode Island. Young Constance, meanwhile, attended the Lincoln School just "a short walk from her home. There she contributed to "Lincoln Green" and published poetry and fiction. She acted in productions and played on the baseball and basketball teams."

Following her junior year, Constance decided to spend the summer vacationing in Europe with the family of her mother's cousin Isaac Peace Hazard II. She enjoyed the sites of Europe, but, being an athletic girl, wanted to engage in a more strenuous activity.

On a bright August day, Constance decided to climb the Swiss Alps. By day's end she felt pretty tired, nothing unusual perhaps after such a strenuous day. The next morning, however, she awoke with a slight fever, a condition that only worsened over the next few days. Thought to be the common cold, the fifteen year old was seen by a

Swiss doctor who diagnosed the girl who had always enjoyed good health, with a failing heart. Just a few days later the vibrant, athletic and talented adolescent girl lay dead from a heart attack suffered on August 30, 1929, just 6 days short of her 16th birthday. She was buried in Saas Fee, Switzerland.

Rather than greeting her daughter upon her expected return to Providence planned for early September, Dorothy received a cablegram informing her of her young daughter's death. The grief stricken woman telephoned her sister, Mrs. Martin H. Knapp of Syracuse and Cazenovia, almost immediately thereafter.

As the months passed, the Hunts began to think of ways to memorialize young Constance. In 1930 Dorothy "collected her [daughter's] poems and had them printed in a limited edition for Constance's friends and family as *Sunshine and Stardust*."[29]

She and her husband also purchased a 69,000 square foot piece of land, a former dumping ground at 210 Pitman Street opposite their home between Waterman and Pitman Streets. At the same time they commissioned New York Sculptor Gail Sherman Corbett, a student of Augustus Saint Gaudens, one of the most important American sculptors of the nineteenth century, to design a statue. Though the statue is not a portrait of Constance, it does capture her whimsical youth and spirit. Corbett's husband, Wiley Corbett, architect of the Metropolitan Life Building in New York, designed the base for the bronze which was cast by the Gorham Manufacturing Company. On the base are inscribed the words from one of Constance's poems that may have epitomized her free spirit, "THE WIND ROARS BY, I FEEL IT BLOW, AND KNOW THAT I AM FREE TO GO."

The statue and the new park, named by the City in the girl's honor, were dedicated on November 16, 1933. The former dumping ground became the Constance Witherby Park, a lush open green space with a few carefully placed park benches. An additional 30,000 square feet of land was added to the park in 1930, another donation made by the Hunts.

---

[29]Rhode Island Historical Society Manuscripts Division, Introduction to the Witherby Family Papers, Processed by Rick Stattler, October 1999.

The statue stood in the Constance Witherby Park largely unnoticed until the spring of 1992 when it was vandalized by malcontents who sawed off and stole its arms. City officials decided to restore the work, remove it from the relatively isolated Pitman Street Park and relocate it to a busier, more central location.

The statue now rests tucked away in a grove of trees just off the trail of the park on Blackstone Boulevard at Clarenden Street. Over 600 bulbs have been planted in the clearing around it and they make a beautiful spring bloom that Constance herself would have enjoyed. The Statuary Conservation of Lincoln replaced the arms, cleaned the work and applied a protective coating at a cost of about $14,000.

Parks Commissioner Nancy Derrig noted at the time, "People just love it. She really is spectacular. More people have seen the statue of Constance Witherby in the last month than probably have seen it since 1933."

In 1925, Constance penned a poem she called WISH. That poem perhaps foreshadowed her immortalization in this location. She wrote,

"I wish I could see a mermaid fair,
With a glistening crown of pearls,
I wish I could see a fountain played
In the moonlight, falling in swirls.
I wish I could see a fairy spray
Of tinkling, merry, flower bells,
I wish I could have a happy day
In the quietest of shady dells.
I wish I could hear a bird's gay song,
The rustling of poplars at home,
I wish I could take a journey long,
Or by the seaside roam.
Oh, I wish I could do what I want to do,
And have what I want to have."

● ● ●

Though taken from the world all too soon, Constance's spirit lives on in both her poems and her statue that now watches the walkers, runners and bikers pass by her as she stands in the *"quietest of shady dells."*

Chapter 29

Abbott Park

Broad Street at the corner of Chestnut Street

ABBOTT PARK FOUNTAIN

Born in 1682, Daniel Abbott donated what, at the time, was the largest donation of land to Providence until the Betsy Williams 102 acre donation of what is now Roger Williams Park. In 1873 the exquisite Abbott Fountain was erected as the focal point of Abbott Park fronting on Broad St. at Chestnut. (Photo by Paul Caranci)

THE FREEDOM BELL

Abbott Park was also the site of the July 5, 1999 gathering of a group of Church and community people in an act of repentance for African American slavery and in celebration of human freedom. The Freedom Bell, situated just behind the Abbott Fountain, now observes the spot. (Photo by Paul Caranci)

Daniel Abbott was born on April 8, 1682 to Daniel and Margaret (White) Abbott and was both an early and prominent resident of Providence. He worked as an attorney and was apparently a man of significant wealth and stature. In 1723 Abbott and his wife Mary (Fenner) donated a parcel of land for the establishment of a Presbyterian or Congregational church. Twenty three years later he conveyed to a committee of the Congregational society a 7,000 square feet parcel of land designated for the public use, "always to be kept free and clear of any building, fencing or other encumbrance to the prejudice of the public forever."[30] That land at 290 Weybosset Street became the City's first park and would remain the only public park on land donated by a resident until the 1871 donation by Betsy Williams of 102 acres of farmland and woodland that is now known as Roger Williams Park.

In 1733 Abbott was appointed by the Assembly to construct a new jail in the city and a few years later was elected to serve as the Rhode Island Colony's 24th Deputy Governor holding office from July 1738 to May 1740. He also served as Deputy, Speaker of the House of Deputies and Clerk of the Assembly.

In 1873 a fountain was erected as a focal point of the park area. It was originally surrounded by a fence which has since been dismantled. The property fronting on Broad Street near Chestnut has been in constant use as a park since then.

Abbott died in his 78th year on November 7, 1760 and is buried in the North Burial Ground. Abbott Park continues to serve as a permanent testimonial of his contributions to Providence.

Immediately behind the Abbott Fountain is a smaller monument totally unrelated to the Fountain, but still meritorious of a mention. The Freedom Bell marks the spot where a group of Church and community people gathered in an act of repentance for African American slavery and in celebration of human freedom. The gathering was held on July 5, 1999 in conjunction with the 22nd General Synod of the United Church of Christ.

---

[30]The Narragansett Historical Register – Vol. 6 – James N Arnold, editor. – A facsimile reprint – published in 1996 by Heritage Books, Inc., Bowie, MD., p. 85.

Chapter 30

Gano St. Park

aka Slate Rock Park

East Transit Street
Corner of Gano and Power Streets

ROGER WILLIAMS LANDING PLACE

When Roger Williams fled Massachusetts in 1636, his travel took him across the Seekonk River to the shore of Rhode Island. As he stepped from his canoe, he was welcomed by members of the Narragansett Indian tribe with the greeting, "What Cheer Netop!" The Roger Williams Landing Place monument marks the spot where Williams first step foot on Rhode Island soil. (Photo courtesy of the Rhode Island State Archives, Preston Collection, C#858)

When Roger Williams was banished from Massachusetts his followers fled south toward a vast wilderness inhabited only by members of the Narragansett Indian tribe. Eventually crossing the Seekonk River in a canoe, Williams stepped upon a slate rock to the Indian greeting, "What cheer, Netop."

Since the 1877 development of Gano Street, the area where Williams landed is no longer at the River's edge, and the actual slate rock on which Williams' stepped was accidentally destroyed by a 1877 dynamite blast intended to save it.

The Association of Merchants and Manufacturers gifted this monument to the City. It was dedicated in 1906 and rededicated in 1989 when it was restored by the Healy Brothers Foundry in Lincoln. The stone, designed by Frank Foster Tingley and crafted by Alonzo

• • •

Chappel is made from pink Westerly granite and stands slightly less than eleven feet tall. Originally, four bronze tablets, depicting Roger Williams landing and being greeted by Narragansett Indians were cast by the Gorham Company and set into the stone, but they have since been removed. The monument stands in Slate Rock Park at the corner of Gano and Power Streets.

Chapter 31

Columbus Park

Intersection of Reservoir Avenue and Elmwood Avenue

CHRISTOPHER COLUMBUS

Though credited with discovering the continent of North America, Christopher Columbus never actually stepped foot on the continent. Rather he landed in the modern day island of Bahama thinking he had sailed to India. (Photo courtesy of the Rhode Island State Archives, Preston Collection, C#858)

Renowned sculptor Frederic Auguste Bartholdi, whose works include the Statue of Liberty, was commissioned to design a statue of Christopher Columbus for The World's Columbian Exposition that was held in Chicago in 1892. Bartholdi had his creation cast at the Gorham Manufacturing Company in sterling silver as a demonstration of the company's skills. A year later, the statue was recast in bronze and dedicated in a grassy triangle at the intersection of Reservoir and Elmwood Avenues in the City's West End. Elmwood Avenue was then home to many of Providence's most opulent families and it was the Elmwood Association that gifted the statue to the City which dedicated it on November 8, 1893.

Born in 1451 in a seaside village near Genoa, Italy, Columbus began sailing as a teenager. As a young adult he believed that sailing west would provide a speedier passage to India. Portugal rejected the idea, but the notion intrigued the King and Queen of Spain, who in August 1492 financed his passage west. Two months later he landed on the island known today as Bahama. He also traveled to Hispaniola, modern day Haiti and Dominican Republic. Columbus mistakenly thought he landed in India. Either way, he never set foot on the continent of North America as is widely believed, though his discovery in many ways still changed the course of history.

The statue depicts Columbus the navigator in full length standing on a granite base holding a sphere in his left hand. Looking to the right, Columbus' right arm is extended with his index finger pointing outward. The statue of Columbus stands 6' tall and he is wearing period cloths with his open coat blowing in an imaginary breeze. At his right foot is a length of rope rolled and neatly piled on top of an anchor. In 2001 the statue was placed on the National Register of Historic Places.

Chapter 32

Lippitt Park

1015 Hope Street near the Pawtucket city line

ANTHONY MEMORIAL FOUNTAIN

Henry Bowen Anthony was the powerful owner/editor of the Providence Journal and later served 25 years in the United States Senate. Upon his death he left the City $35,000 to establish a fountain in his memory. Controversy surrounded its siting, but the Anthony Memorial Fountain was eventually placed in Lippitt Park as a favor to the Ward 2 councilman. (Photo byPaul Caranci)

Upon his passing Henry Bowen Anthony left the City the sum of $35,000 to establish a fountain in his memory. The mid-19th century owner/editor of the Providence Journal and Rhode Island's United States Senator from 1859 to 1884 left specific instructions on the placement of the fountain. It was to be located either on Prospect Terrace or in the North Burial Ground. After much deliberation, the City Council rejected both "suggestions" as an apparent favor to a councilman who lobbied for placement in the Ward 2 area that he represented.

In 1939, the council finally announced that the memorial would be located on land donated in 1933 by Swan Point Cemetery.

The resulting park was named in honor of World War I veteran Alexander Farnum Lippit who gave his life in the war and whose family was very close to Anthony's family.

The granite fountain is crafted in the Moderne style and represents the design of Jackson, Robertson, and Adams. A prominent vertical thrust at the fountain's center rises from four hemispherical basins in the center forming a nice contrast of geometric shapes classic of the style. The memorial park is located on Hope Street at the Providence and Pawtucket border.

Chapter 33

Davis Park

700 Chalkstone Avenue

CESAR CHAVEZ

Cesar Chavez worked indefatigably for the rights of migrant workers. He always advocated and employed non-violent means of bringing attention to his cause. These included marches, boycotts and hunger strikes, including one that lasted 36 days. (Photo by Paul Caranci)

● ● ●

Born near Yuma, Arizona on March 31, 1927, Cesario Estrada Chavez learned early that the life of a migrant farm worker was difficult. Young Cesar and his family worked the fields for long hours under oppressive conditions. For that reason Chavez dedicated his life to improving the workers conditions, pay and treatment.

Throughout the 1950s, Chavez worked as a community and labor organizer. He founded the National Farm Workers Association in the early 1960s helping to organize the first strike against California grape growers in 1965. His efforts resulted in several worker victories and signed contracts between the workers and the growers.

In 1972 his union merged with the Agricultural Workers Organizing Committee and the two became known as the United Farm Workers. Though greater in number, the members faced significant challenges even from other unions such as the Teamsters.

Chavez always advocated and employed non-violent means of bringing attention to his cause. These included marches, boycotts and hunger strikes, including one that lasted 36 days. Though effective, a hunger strike may have contributed to his death which came in San Luis, Arizona on April 23, 1993. Chavez was 65 and his birthday has become a holiday in California, Colorado and Texas. He has been honored with a postage stamp and in statue. Streets are named for him and President Barack Obama proclaimed March 31 "Cesar Chavez Day" in the United States.

In May 2006, the Providence Board of Contract and Supply approved the expenditure of $12,500 to the Urban League of Rhode Island for a bronze statue of Chavez for installation at Davis Park. The remaining $12,500 needed to design and cast the statue was raised privately by a memorial committee.

On November 6, 2007, Chavez's granddaughter visited Providence City Hall to view the statue of her grandfather that was being housed there until construction was complete at its permanent home at Davis Park on Chalkstone Avenue in Providence. The statue was also displayed in ceremony on March 27, 2009 at the State House prior to its dedication in Davis Park. The bronze statue rests on an unfinished granite rock and depicts Chavez wearing work shirt and pants with his right hand raised over his head as if waving to an imaginary crowd of people. His left arm is hanging low at his side and with his left hand he holds a couple of books.

• • •

Chapter 34

Memorial Park
War Veterans Park

Intersection of Memorial Boulevard and South Main Street

WORLD WAR I MONUMENT

In 1929 Providence erected what is still its tallest memorial - the World War I Monument. Topped with the bronze statue of a woman representing the heroic figure of peace, the fluted granite shaft stands 150' tall. (Photo courtesy of the Rhode Island State Archives, Preston Collection, C#858)

She sits atop one of the tallest of the City's monuments keeping a watchful eye over the Providence River, casting a long shadow on the Licht Judicial Center behind her. She represents a heroic figure of Peace and adorns the 150' tall, fluted, Westerly granite column that was erected in 1929 as a memorial to the Rhode Island soldiers who defended our freedom in the First World War.

At its polygonal base are steps leading to the shaft from every direction. The first step is decorated with bronze panels depicting ships, planes, etc. The plinth contains four large faces inscribed with words from the City's dedication of the monument and quotes from Lincoln, Wilson and Emerson. Between each face is an insignia of a different branch of military service.

• • •

The lower part of the column contains a memorial frieze (base) representing the virtues of the Rhode Islanders that participated in the war effort. The names of all the major battles of the War in which they fought are emblazoned above the frieze, the ornamental sculptured band that horizontally encircles the shaft.

The monument was commissioned by the City of Providence and the design was the result of a competition won by architect Paul Cret whose other local designs include the football stadium at Brown University. The female figure of Peace was designed by Paul C. Jennewein and sculpted by Italian sculptor Vincenzo Fiorito.

WORLD WAR II MONUMENT

Sixty two years in the making, the World War II Monument embodies the conception of World War II and Korean War veteran Joseph T. Corrente of Cranston. The multi-faceted monument honors the 96,000 Rhode Island men and woman who contributed to the war effort and was dedicated in 2007. (Photo by Heather Caranci)

In the green open space just south of the World War I Monument is another of the Park's monuments, this one honoring the 96,000 local men and women of World War II. Dedicated on November 11, 2007, this circular colonnade is 16 feet in diameter and has eight round granite columns each measuring fourteen feet in height and spaced at a distance of three feet.

The granite floor within the columns depicts a Mercator map (flat map of the world). Numbers on the map reference the war's major battles which are inscribed on the inside face of the column bases.

Capping the monument is a 4' wide granite capital and cornice bringing the total height of the monument to eighteen feet. The monument is surrounded by a granite circular retaining wall measuring three feet high on which are displayed the crests of all 39 Rhode

Island municipalities. Two granite pylon walls containing an honor roll of the 2,560 Rhode Islanders who died in the conflict flank the entrance. Finally, four contemplation benches are stationed in front of the honor roll, two in front of each wall allowing visitors to view the inscribed names of those who made the ultimate sacrifice for their state and country. Each bench is inscribed with one of four freedoms; freedom of speech and expression, freedom of worship, freedom from want and freedom from fear. A granite stone embedded on the monument's floor reads, "This monument is dedicated to the men and women of Rhode Island who served and those who died in the struggle to establish a world founded upon the four freedoms cited by Franklin D. Roosevelt in his address to Congress on January 6, 1941."

The monument embodies the conception of World War II and Korean War veteran Joseph T. Corrente of Cranston, RI who was a major driving force in the monument's construction. Professional services were provided by Paul Cavanaugh.

KOREAN WAR MEMORIAL

The Korean War Memorial was designed to represent the spirit of service, the willingness of sacrifice and the dedication to the cause of freedom that characterized all of the participants of that war. The memorial was dedicated in 1998 in tribute to the 39,000 Rhode Islanders who served the nation during that conflict. (Photo by Heather Caranci)

Mayor Vincent A. (Buddy) Cianci, Jr. established the Korean War Memorial Commission in 1995 to determine the proper way of expressing Rhode Island's everlasting gratitude to those who sacrificed for our nation in the Korean War. Designed to represent the spirit of service, the willingness of sacrifice, and the dedication to the cause of freedom that characterized all of the participants, the resulting monument was dedicated on October 8, 1998 in tribute to those 39,000 Rhode Islanders who served during that conflict.

The centerpiece of the memorial is a sculpture of a soldier. He kneels low with his head covered by a hood in an effort to stave off the bitter cold and frigid wind. His head is down but he clutches his rifle in his hands keeping it at the ready. He conveys a feeling of loneliness and being forgotten yet deep loyalty to his country. (Some call the Korean War the "Forgotten War" because few understood the impact of the war and few cared.)

The statue created by Robert Shure is cast in bronze. It is surrounded by a walkway of white brick engraved with the names of the 145 Rhode Islanders who were killed in action and the 55 still listed as missing in action. In addition, red bricks commemorate those war veterans remembered by friends and family. The sale of the red bricks provided the main source of revenue for the project.

World War II and Korean War veteran Theodore F. Low served as chairman of the Memorial Commission and a major impetus of the project.

Conclusion

The expansive yet distinct nature and breadth of statuary, monuments, memorials and sculpture should be apparent by now. They dot the landscape, telling stories and evoking emotion. Individually they are diverse, designed with singular purpose in mind. Collectively they are distinctive in detail yet compelling in nature as they recall loves lost, lands discovered, battles won and the horrors of war. They tell tales, spin yarns, expose us to mythology, recount history, recall heroes, and paint pictures of both uncommon valor and unusual behavior. They capture joy and pain, heartache and sorrow, euphoria and disappointment. Yet each is a masterpiece of art.

Seductive in beauty, statues, sculptures, monuments and memorials are often noticed but just as often overlooked as we go about our daily routine. But one day something *compels* you to take notice. That's the "ahhh" moment of discovery and wonderment; when did that statue appear? Or what is that supposed to be? are questions typically asked, even if to one's self, as our brain focuses on what our eye has finally taken the time to see?

Every statue, monument, memorial and sculpture has a story. Hopefully, now that you know what that story is you will take the time to look at each piece again, or scout it out for the very first time, and, if only for a moment, find yourself back in time, seeing the sites, hearing the voices and taking in the scents that these extraordinary works of art have frozen in time.

• • •

Afterword

In this book, *Monumental Providence*, Paul Caranci, prolific historian and Rhode Island's deputy secretary of state, and his daughter Heather have performed a monumental task in identifying the sculptures and monuments of the capital city. Their cultural odyssey has taken them to every part of our 18.91 square mile metropolis to locate and identify these works of art. Their inventory describes not only the object itself, but what it represents. It contains histories of the people who are honored, information on the craftsmen who created the artifacts, discussions of the symbolic nature of certain works of art, and, where appropriate, acknowledgment of the public-spirited citizens who donated these artworks for all to view and appreciate.

The Carancis' work not only updates an earlier book entitled *Hidden Treasure* (1980) by Vivienne Lasky and Robert Freeman, it is also broader in scope, especially as it pertains to Providence College and the neighborhoods; and it contains more depth and detail.

As an historic American city, the birthplace of church-state separation, the seat of prestigious institutions of higher education, the state capital, and a place of wide ethno-cultural diversity, Providence is the perfect subject for the book Paul and Heather have compiled. They have given us not only an artistic tour of the city, they have written a book that is a *tour de force*.

Patrick T. Conley
Historian Laureate of Rhode Island

Bibliography

Books

Arnold, James N. *The Narragansett Historical Register – Vol. 6 –* James N Arnold, editor. – A facsimile reprint. Bowie, MD, Heritage Books, Inc., 1996

Chaput, Erik J. *The People's Martyr: Thomas Wilson Dorr and His 1842 Rhode Island Rebellion.* Lawrence, University of Kansas Press, 2013

Cook, Rodney Mims Jr. *Atlanta's Parks and Monuments - Image of America Series.* Charleston, Arcadia Publishing, 2013

Freeman, Robert and Lasky, Vivienne. *Hidden Treasure: Public Sculpture in Providence.* Providence: The Rhode Island Publication Society by the Rhode Island Bicentennial Foundation, 1980

Historical Preservation & Heritage Commission, Rhode Island. *Outdoor Sculpture of Rhode Island.* Providence: RI Historical Preservation & Heritage Commission, 1999

McGowan, Louis and Brown, Daniel. *Providence - Postcard History Series.* Charleston, Arcadia Publishing, 2006

Providence, City of. *Dedication of the Equestrian Statue of Major General Ambrose E. Burnside, July 4, 1887, With the Oration of General Horatio Rogers,* E.L. Freeman & Sons, Printers & Publishers, 1887

Sampson, Amory Chapin. *Daniel Wanton Lyman 1844-1886 An Appreciation.* Providence, Standard Printing Company, 1913

Wiggins, Dr. David N. *Georgia's Confederate Monuments and Cemeteries – Image of America Series.* Charleston, Arcadia Publishing, 2006

Internet Sources

Babcock-Smith House Museum Website. "Westerly Granite in Rhode Island – Civil War Monuments, Providence Soldiers' and Sailors' Monument." http://www.babcock-smithhouse.com/

Biographies

"Christiana Cateaux Bannister." http://www.Edward bannister.com/biographies/cbbio.html

Biography Website. *"Giuseppe Garibaldi: Folk Hero, Military Leader (1807-1882)."* http://www.biography.com/

Blackstone Daily.com. "A Reflection of Slavery, Freedom, and a Blackstone Valley Abolitionist" by Diane Marie Mariani. http://www.blackstonedaily.com/Journeys/elizabethbuffum-chace.htm

Blackstone Parks Conservancy Website. http://www. Blackstone parksconservancy.org/

Blog Daily Herald. *"Art School(ed): A Useful Ranking of the Ivy League's Henry Moore Sculptures."* By Edith Young, November 16, 2013. http://blogdailyherald.com/2013/11/16/art-schooled-useful-ranking-ivy-leagues-henry-moore-sculptures/

Brown University Website. http://www.brown.edu/cis/sta/dev/prov idence_architecture/locations/downtown/turks_head_building/ http://www.brown.edu/about/public-art/gifts/henry-moore-reclining-figureno2bridgeprop1963http://www.brown.edu/about/publicart/col-lectionhttp://www.brown.edu/cis/sta/dev/providence_architecture/lo-cations/college_hill/sullivan_dorr_house/ http://library.brown.edu/guide/07.htmlhttps://repository.li-brary.brown.edu/studio/search_results?search_terms=terms=Ab-bate/%20Pablo%20S.'&scope=Search/2013/10/26/catherine-teitz-14-classical-statues *"Catherine Teitz '14: Classical Statues of Brown University.*October26,2013byAndyDuf-ton.https://blogs.brown.edu/archaeology250

* * *

Callums, George W. "Biographical Register of the Officers and Graduates of the United States Military Academy at West Point, New York, since its establishment in 1802." http://penelope.uchicago.edu/Thayer/E/Gazetteer/Places/America/United_States/Army/USMA/Cullums_Register/1348*.html

Chambers, William Paris. *"Well-Known Soloists from All Walks of Life."* http://www.angelfire.com/music2/thecornetcompendium/well_known_soloists_3.html

City of Providence Website. "Providence City Hall Construction Records18741879RG211" https://www.providenceri.com/print/archives/providence-city-hall-constructiion-records-0

Cyclopaedia.net. *"AskMrKnowItAllD.WReeves"* http://www.cyclopaedia.info/wiki/D.-W.-Reeves

deCordova Sculpture Park and Museum Website. "Group of Three, the Pembroke Piece." By Hugh Townley http://www.decordova.org/art/sculpture-park/group-three-pembroke-piece

Ecology of Culture Blog. Benjamin Franklin (1858) - RI's 1st Public Sculpture. Last Seen in 2000 by Nancy Austin, PhD. Saturday, September 11, 2010. http://ecologyofculture.blogspot.com/2010/09 /benjamin-franklin-1858-ris-1st-public.html

Encyclopedia.com. "Garibaldi,Giuseppe" 2006. http://www.encyclopedia.com/article-1G2-3446900336/garibaldi-giuseppe.html

EWTN Website. *"St. Michael-Archangel, Feast: September 29."* http://www.ewtn.com/library/mary/michael.htm

Geocaching.com Website. "Providence War Memorials." http://www.geocaching.com/geocache/GC1Z8A2_providence-war-memorials

Good Night Irene Productions Website. http://goodnightirene productions.com/men_trailer.html

I Heart Rhody Website. Sights – *"The Turk's Head Building – Providence."* http://www.iheartrhody.com/2012/11/sights-turks-head-building-providence-html http://www.iheartrhody.com/2012/04/sights-s75-al-america-one-by-dusan.html

Irish Famine Memorial Website. http://www.rifamine memorial.com/rifamine.html

Johnson & Wales University Website. Transformational Leaders: Morris J.W. Gaebe. http://www.jwu.edu/newsletter.aspx? pageid=965549

Johnson & Wales University Website. Making History: From Business School to Junior College. http://www.jwu.edu/ content.aspx?id=965521

Korean War Memorial of Rhode Island Website. http://rikorean warmemorial.com/about.php

Martha Mitchell's Encyclopedia Brunoniana. *"Bridge-Prop."* http://www.brown.edu/Administration/News_Bureau/Databases/Encyclopedia/search.php?serial=B0350

Martha Mitchell's Encyclopedia Brunoniana. *"Dante"* http://www.brown.edu/administration/News_Bureau/databases/Encyclopedia/search.php?serial=Do

Martha Mitchell's Encyclopedia Brunoniana. *"Caesar Augustus" http://www.brown.edu.Administration.News_Bureau/Databases/Encyclopedia/search.php?serial+Co*

Pablo Eduardo Sculptor Website. *"Resume."* http://www.pablo eduardosculpture.com/biography/resume/

Providence Athenaeum Webstie. Fascinating Facts. *"Fountain of Legend."* http://www.providenceathenaeum.ort/facts/facts.html

Rhode Island PBS Website. "Bird on the Wire," February 23, 2011, http://rhodeislandpbs.blogspot.com/2011/02/rhode-island-stories-features-film.html

RI State Council on the Arts Website – *"Providence Public Art. "Bearing Figure,"*Sunday, April 27, 2014. http://www.arts.ri.gov/publicart/ArtDetail.php?art_id=11

Providence College Website. *"Providence College War Memorial Grotto. "*http://library.providence.edu/spcol/grotto/exhibits/show/grotto

Providence Public Library Website. *"Roger Williams Park"* David Wallis Reeves Fountain. http://www.prov.ib.org/ imagecollections/rhodeislandimagecollection/rogerwilliamspark?page=7 and http://www/provlib.org/roger-williams-park/david-wallis-reeves-fountain image 89 of 91.

Providence Rotary Website, Community Service. *"Roger Williams Park Fountain"* http://www.providencerotary.orgCommunity Service.cfm?print=n

PublicArtArchive.*"BearingFigure"* http://www.publicartarchive.org/work/bearing-figure

Quahog.org Website Attractions. *"Rhode Island State House: A Defective Cannon, a Fake Liberty Bell, Some Moon Dust, and a Convicted Felon."* http://www.quahog.org/attractions/ index.php?id=62

Quahog.org Website Facts and Folklore. *"Elizabeth Buffum Chace and Lillie Chace Wyman: Unstoppable Mother and Daughter Activists"*by Elizabeth C. Stevens. http://www.quahog.org/ factsfolklore/index.php?id=104

Quahog.org Website Facts and Folklore. *"Theodore Francis Green: The Story of His Resignation From the United States Senate"* by Florence Markoff. http://www.quahog.org/factsfolklore/ index.php?id=51

• • •

Questia Trusted Online Research. Providence – *"There's a Story Be-hind Every Statue"* from a Providence Journal story by Tatiana Pina. http://www.questia.com/newspaper/1P236706113/providence-there-s-a-story-behind-every-statue

Roadside America Website. *"Tree Root That Ate Roger Williams."* http://www.roadsideamerica.com/story/2210

Rhode Island Archival and Manuscript Collections Online. *Brown and Ives Records.* http://riamco.org/render.php?eadid=US-RPJCB-ms7&view=biography

Rhode Island Heritage Hall of Fame Website. *"Inductees – Christiana Carteaux Bannister"* http://www.riheritagehalloffame.ort/ inductees_detail.cfm?iid=466

Saint Michael the archangel Website. http://www.stmichaelsprov.org/

Skylight Studios, Inc. Website. The Founders of Johnson & Wales University Providence, RI. http://www.skylightstudios.inc.com/e/sculpture-for-schools-colleges-universities/

Smithsonian Institution. *"Collections Search Center"* http://collections.si.edu/search/results.htm?q=Outdoor%20Sculpture&fq=text:Rhode%20Island&fq=text:Providence

Strange New England, A Field Guide to New England Legends, Curious History, and Weird Destinations Website. *"Turks Head."* http://strangene.com/landmarks/turks.htm

Waymarking.com Website. "World War I Memorial – Providence, RI,"http://www.waymarking.com/way-marks/WM57FY_World_War_I_Memorial_Providence,RI

Wikipedia."J.HowardMcGrath"http://en.wikipedia.org/wiki/J._Howard_McGrath

Wikipedia.*"Sri Chinmoy"* http://en.wikipedia.org/wiki/Sri_Chinmoy

Wikipedia. *"Francis. Wayland"* http://en.wikipedia.org/wiki/ Francis_Wayland

World Black History. *Christiana Barteaux Bannister (1899-1902).* April 23, 2013. http://wwwmrhall.blogspot.com/2013/04/christiana-carteaux-bannister_23.html

World War II Memorial Website. http://www/riwwii memorial.org/aboutme.htm

Periodicals

Anchor, The. *Rivalry of Anchor Goes Back to 1928.* Rhode Island College Newspaper, November 17, 1959.

American Society of Composers, Authors and Poets (ASCAP) Website. *"Commemorating Cohan – 'Yankee Doodle Boy' Writer and ASCAP Co-founder to Get Statue in Providence, RI.* July 7, 2009. http://www.ascap.com/playback/2009/spring/action/cohan.aspx?print=1

American Society of Composers, Authors and Poets (ASCAP) Website. *"George M. Cohan Statue Unveiled in Providence, RI."* August19,009.http://www.ascap.com/playback/2009/08/action/cohan_statue_unveiled.aspx

Borg, Linda. *"A Garden of Memories – Ceremony Honors Two R.I. Soldiers Who Died in Iraq."* The Providence Journal, July 29, 2007.

Coelho, Courtney. *"Circle Dance: Gift of Art Coming to Brown."* Brown Daily Herald, November 19, 2012.

Dujardin, Richard C. *"Fire Destroys Carriage House That Was to Become Fire Museum."* The Providence Journal, April 15, 2009.

Gray, Channing. *Four-Ton Statue Gets Walking Papers.* The Arts Column, Providence Journal Bulletin, April 23, 1984.

Hill, John. *"Westerly Granite Found in Hundreds of Monuments, From Gettysburg to Roger Williams Statue."* The Providence Journal, October 5, 2013

Jordon, Jennifer D. *"The Garden of Heroes – Memorial to Dead is Dedicated."* Providence Journal/Evening Bulletin, October 24, 2005.

JWU. *"Pioneers,"* Johnson & Wales University Magazine, Fall 2013.

Lennon, Sheila. *"Time Lapse: 'America Militant' Thinks She's Watching a First; Is She Right? When, Where, What's Happening?* The Providence Journal, May 25, 2014.

Morgan, Thomas J. "State House Statue Commemorates Defiant Dorr's Contributions To R.I." Providence Journal, January 7, 2014.

Margolis, Rachel. *'"Circle Dance' Sculpture Set to Arrive on the Walk."* Brown Daily Herald, November 6, 2012

New York Times, The. *"George M. Cohan, 64, Dies at Home Here."* Obitiuary, November 6, 1942

Patinkin, Mark. *"To University Chancellor, 'Fun is A Valuable Career Skill."* The Providence Journal, January 19, 1997

Raub, Patricia. *"Burnside: Our Statue But Not Our Hero."* Occupied Providence Journal, February 21, 2012

Rhode Island Historical Preservation Commission. *"Application to the United States Department of the Interior National Park Service for the inclusion of the Roger Williams Park Historic District on the National Register of Historic Places."* 1974

Rhode Island Historical Society Manuscripts Division, *"Introduction to the Witherby Family Papers."* Processed by Rick Stattler, October 1999

Rhode Island Catholic, The, Obituary. "Msgr. Galliano J. Cavallaro" March 11, 2010

Roman Catholic Bishop of Providence. "*Application to the United States Department of the Interior National Park Service for the inclusion of St. Michael's Roman Catholic Church, Convent, Rectory and School on the National Register of Historic Places.*"1975

Van Siclen, Bill. "*Tour Brown University's Beauty in Art and Architecture.*" The Providence Journal, May 22, 2014.

Van Siclen, Bill. "*An Iron and Stone, School Acknowledges Slave Ties.*" The Providence Journal, September 21, 2014.

Reports

Tercentenary Commission, Rhode Island. *Rhode Island Tercentenary 1636 – 1936.* Providence: State of Rhode Island and Providence Plantations Tercentenary Commission, 1937

Rhode Island Historical Society Executive Board and the Secretary of State. *Report of Committee on Marking Historical Sites in Rhode Island Made to the General Assembly.* Providence: E.L Freeman Company, 1914

About the Authors

Casey, the 5 year-old son of author Heather Caranci, sits atop Sentinal, the iconic statue of the heroic mastiff that saved two lives during the 1849 East Side fire that claimed two others. He is pictured with the book's co-authors, Paul F. and Heather A. Caranci.

Paul F. Caranci has served as Rhode Island's Deputy Secretary of State since 2007. He is a historian and serves on the boards of directors for the RI Heritage Hall of Fame and the Heritage Harbor Museum. He is a co-founder of, and consultant to The Municipal Heritage Group and the author of four published books including two produced by The History Press. North Providence: A History & The People Who Shaped It (2012) and The Hanging & Redemption of John Gordon: The True Story of Rhode Island's Last Execution (2013). He is married to his high school sweetheart, Margie and makes his home in North Providence. The couple has two adult children, Heather and Matthew and four grandsons, Matthew Jr., Jacob, Vincent and Casey.

Heather A. Caranci is a history enthusiast who serves on the board of directors of The Municipal Heritage Group. She attended Roger Williams University and is currently employed at Conley Casting Supply Corp. She and her son Casey make their home in North Providence. This is her first book

Made in the USA
Middletown, DE
28 January 2015